THE PILLAR

THE PILLAR

The Life and Afterlife
of the Nelson Pillar

Donal Fallon

NEW ISLAND

THE PILLAR
First published 2014
by New Island Books
16 Priory Office Park
Stillorgan
County Dublin

www.newisland.ie

PRINT ISBN: 978-1-84840-326-0
EPUB ISBN: 978-1-84840-327-7
MOBI ISBN: 978-1-84840-338-4

Every effort has been made to contact and credit the owners of the images in this work.

Typeset by JVR Creative India
Printed by ScandBook AB, Sweden

10 9 8 7 6 5 4 3 2 1

We'll even climb the Pillar like you always meant to,
Watch the sun rise over the strand.
Close your eyes and we'll pretend,
It could somehow be the same again.

– Phil Chevron, 'Song of the Faithful Departed'
(Courtesy of Rockin' Music)

To Shane MacThomáis.
A gifted historian and a true Dubliner.

Contents

Acknowledgements

T here are a great many people without whom this publication would not be here.

In very challenging times, immense thanks and praise are due to the staff of the various archives and libraries I utilised in the course of this work, who continue to do fantastic work for the cultural benefit of the Irish people. I owe a great debt of thanks to all at the National Library of Ireland, the Dublin City Library and Archive, Military Archives, the Irish Architectural Archive, UCD Library and the National Archives of Ireland.

Individuals who donated pictures and stories to this work also have my sincere gratitude. Any history of the Nelson Pillar depends on strong visual content, and many people assisted on that front. In particular I'd like to thank Pól Ó Duibhir, who allowed me free reign with his brilliant images from the aftermath of both the republican bombing and the Irish Army-controlled demolition, as well as shots taken during the lifetime of the pillar. He has contributed much to this work by allowing these pictures to appear in print for the first time.

Paul Reynolds was willing to provide images for this work, as he did for the *Come Here To Me!* book in 2012, and I thank him again for his continued support. Joe Saunders, Brenda Armstrong Kelleher, Margaret Nugent, Orla Fitzpatrick, Niall McCormack and many others who helped me with sourcing material for the book deserve great thanks. Franc Myles deserves thanks too for sharing with me his memories of working on the excavation of the site of the pillar in 2001, prior to the placement of the Spire there.

Sam and Ciaran from *Come Here To Me!* have always supported me along the way, as have many other friends, who have listened to me talk about little else but Horatio Nelson for quite some time. Eoin Purcell and all at New Island Books have backed this project as they backed *Come Here To Me!*, and for that I am very grateful.

I am indebted to Mick Healy and Bas Ó Curraoin, who have interviewed several republican veterans of the 1950s and 1960s, including Liam Sutcliffe, who played no small part in the downfall of Horatio Nelson on O'Connell Street. Their footage is a priceless resource for a historian interested in this period.

My family have always had faith in my endeavours, and to my parents and brother I must express enormous gratitude. My partner Aoife has always believed in this and other projects, and for many late nights lost to a laptop, and an ever-increasing stack of books, I can only apologise. I promise to take a break soon.

To all Dubliners who have read my writing on the *Come Here To Me!* website, taken my Adult Education Course at University College Dublin, or just chatted with me about the history of Dublin in the past, thank you for your interest in the history of this wonderful city.

I can be contacted via www.comeheretome.com, and would love to hear from you if you have memories of the pillar, or anything else discussed in this book. Enjoy it.

Donal Fallon,
January 2014.

Eason Collection shot of the Nelson Pillar taken in the 1920s.
Courtesy of the National Library of Ireland.

1. *Before Lord Nelson*

O'Connell Street chimes with history.

A walk down it introduces a visitor to some of the pantheon of Irish nationalist history, ranging from constitutional nationalists like Daniel O'Connell and Charles Stewart Parnell, to the militant socialist Jim Larkin. Now occupied largely by retail space, like so much of the capital, this street began life very differently. As with much of the north inner-city area around it, the eighteenth-century banker and developer Luke Gardiner played a central role in the development of the street. Gardiner had come from very humble beginnings, but as has been noted, 'he became the founder of the family fortune; his combined career as banker, public servant enjoying high office, and speculative property developer made him an influential figure in the civic politics and in the development of Dublin.'[1] Gardiner had been responsible for laying out Henrietta Street in the early 1720s, which rapidly became one of the most exclusive and in-demand housing locations in Dublin, and the work he would commence on what is now O'Connell Street from the 1740s was on an even more impressive scale. Described by James Malton as 'the noblest street in Dublin',[2] what was formerly known as Drogheda Street saw huge changes when Gardiner turned what was once a narrow thoroughfare into a street that commanded attention and respect. Frank Hopkins has noted that:

> He demolished all the original buildings on the street and replaced them with imposing town houses. He doubled the width of the street to 150 feet and erected a tree-lined mall in the centre. The mall was fifty feet wide and 700 feet long and was enclosed by a small wall. Inside the wall there was a pathway lined with elm trees. The mall itself was called Gardiner's Mall and the rest of the street was renamed Sackville Street, after Lionel Caulfield Sackville, first Duke of Dorset and Lord Lieutenant of Ireland from 1731 to 1737 and from 1751 to 1755.[3]

Dublin was a city of many functions in the days of Gardiner. As Siobhán Marie Kilfeather has examined in her cultural history of the Irish capital, Dublin was, in many ways, a city of great importance. It 'had a monopoly of professional services, including higher education and the higher courts of law. As in London, the sittings of parliament became linked to a social season.'[4] S. J. Connolly has detailed how Dublin's predominance in Irish life also came from its economic importance as a major manufacturing centre, with 'large numbers employed in the manufacture of silk and woollen cloth, brewing and distilling, sugar refining, and a variety of luxury trades.'[5] It was a city where political power (limited as it was for much of this period) was centred, and with that it was a city where the landed classes built houses and lived. Some have tended to view this century in an oversimplified manner. It must be acknowledged, however, that alongside this immense wealth was much poverty. Benjamin Franklin, on visiting the city in 1771, had felt compelled to write that while Dublin was a magnificent city in places, 'the appearances of general extreme poverty among the lower people are amazing. They live in wretched hovels of mud and straw, are clothed in rags, and subside largely on potatoes.'[6] We know much about the poverty of parts of eighteenth-century Dublin, thanks to a rather incredible census taken in 1798 by the Protestant Reverend James Whitelaw. As a security measure in light of the recent revolutionary activity, the Lord Mayor of Dublin issued an order to the populace of the city that they would affix a list of inhabitants of each home to the front of their dwellings. With many illiterate in the city, however, this task was given to Reverend Whitelaw, who published some of his findings in 1805, in which he stated:

> I have frequently surprised from ten to 16 persons, of all ages and sexes, in a room, not 15 feet square, stretched on a wad of filthy straw, swarming with vermin, and without any covering, save the wretched rags that constituted their wearing apparel. Under such circumstances, it is not extraordinary that I should have frequently found from 30 to 50 individuals in a house.[7]

If Gardiner's project for Sackville Street was ambitious, it was certainly in keeping with the spirit of the times in Dublin, at least for the prosperous inhabitants. The city saw incredible growth and construction during the eighteenth century, albeit uneven, and centred on the emerging east of the capital. As has been noted, 'extensive, planned urban quarters as well as notable public buildings were almost exclusively to be found downriver from the medieval core.'[8] The magnificent parliament building on College Green, the Royal Exchange (City Hall to us today), the Four Courts building and James Gandon's masterpiece work, the Custom House, are in many ways all monuments still standing to a golden age for the elite.

In addition to these architectural undertakings, the Wide Streets Commission would truly transform parts of Dublin, enhancing the city in a way that would add to its standing and prestige. Its task was to control planning in the city, and to transform a city of alleys into one of streets. The Commissioners operated from the middle of the century, and as Andrew Kincaid has detailed, 'they clearly had a comprehensive vision of the city; they imagined urban space as a planned and controllable unit, but also one that could be manipulated and made to serve several ideologies at once.'[9] The architect Maura Shaffrey has written that:

> ... having begun their work by opening up Parliament Street in 1762, the Commissioners went on to widen Dame Street. Following a grant for this development in 1777, they carried out plans until the end of the century which included the development of Sackville Street.[10]

The widening of Sackville Street was just one contribution to Dublin made by this body, and Lower Sackville Street would bring the street through to the Liffey. By the end of the century the Carlisle Bridge had arrived, linking this impressive northside boulevard with the southside of the Liffey, providing a clear route to the now fashionable and influential College Green. The first stone of the Carlisle Bridge was laid by John Beresford, a relative by marriage to the Gardiner family and a central figure in the history of the Wide Streets Commissioners, on 5 March 1791. The initial bridge was the work of James Gandon, and like Sackville Street it would later see its name changed to honour Daniel O'Connell.

The Vanishing Statue of William Blakeney.

Antique print of William Blakeney.

Saint Patrick's Day of 1759 in Dublin saw the unveiling of a public monument on Sackville Street, an occasion of great pomp and ceremony. This monument was placed in the location that would later be occupied by the Nelson Pillar, making it the first monument on the site. This was also the first statue erected to an Irishman in the capital. Long before Horatio Nelson's exploits at the Battle of Trafalgar, and indeed long before the Spire of Light was even an idea on the table of an architecture firm, hundreds gathered for the unveiling of a statue to William Blakeney. Blakeney, a Limerick man, had been given the freedom of Dublin by the Corporation in 1757, and had a long military career behind him in defence of the Empire. Blakeney had fought at the Siege of Minorca in 1757, when it was captured by the French during the Seven Years' War.

The decision to honour Blakeney with a monument had been made by the Friendly Brothers of Saint Patrick, an organisation that counted a certain Arthur Guinness among its members. Described by Robin Usher as a 'masonic fraternity that opposed duelling and aimed to promote social harmony among the respectable, Catholics (nominally) included',[11] the Friendly Brothers of Saint Patrick frequently met at the Rose Tavern, which was one of the most notable taverns of eighteenth-century Dublin.

J. T. Gilbert writes about the styling of the Friendly Brothers of Saint Patrick in his classic history of the city, first published in the 1850s. He noted that the members wore 'old medals, suspended from a green ribbon, bearing on one side a group of hearts with a celestial crown' and with the motto '*Quis separabit?*' upon them.[12] The society commissioned John Van Nost the Younger to carry out the work, a talented sculptor from a family with a long tradition in the field, and a man whose work can still be seen in Dublin today. The Van Nost family have made significant contributions to the history of sculpture in this city, and the statues of Iustitia (Lady Justice) and Mars in Dublin Castle were also the work of John Van Nost the Younger, placed in their present positions in 1753. Often ridiculed, the statue of Justice faces away from the city of Dublin and gazes inside what was the centre of British administration. A well-known Dublin rhyme joked:

> *The Lady of Justice*
> *Mark well her station*
> *With her face to the Castle*
> *And her arse to the nation.*[13]

The statue of Justice at Dublin Castle today (Image by Ciaran Murray).

A report on the unveiling of the Blakeney statue appeared in the pages of the contemporary magazine *Pue's Occurrences*. Published only days after the unveiling, the magazine noted that:

Last Friday evening the fine Brass Statue of the Right Hon. Lord Blakeney, Knight of the Bath, richly gilded and done by Mr. Van Nost, was carried from his house in Aungier Street, and erected on a superb white marble pedestal in the centre of the Mall in Sackville Street, and Saturday, being St. Patrick's Day, the anniversary festival of that Patron of Ireland, the Grand Knot of the Ancient and Most Benevolent Order of the Friendly Brothers of St. Patrick, assembled in the morning at the Rose Tavern in Castle Street, and, according to annual custom, walked in procession to St. Patrick's Cathedral, where they heard a sermon preached by the Rev. Mr. Benson; after which they proceeded to the Mall where that curious figure was unmasked in the presence of that illustrious body, and amidst unnumbered spectators, amongst whom were many travellers and competent judges of statuary, who declared this performance to be equal, if not superior, to any piece of the kind in Europe, not only for the strength and judgment expressed in the likeness of the brave old original, but also in the beauty and elegance with which the drapery and armour is executed, and which will be a monument to perpetuate the memory of the noble veteran whom it represents, as well as a lasting honour to him and his native country at whose expense it was erected, and which produced a member so worthy of such a reward for his valour, integrity and unshaken fortitude in his eminent services to the King and the public. After the statue was unmasked the Society returned to the Rose, where an elegant entertainment was prepared for their reception.[14]

This statue was all the more remarkable considering its subject was still alive, with Blakeney dying in September 1761. From contemporary sources, it appears that it would fall victim to frequent attack, thrown down from its pedestal and greatly damaged in 1763. Indeed, the monument was so badly damaged that it had to be taken away at the time. The point at which the statue was removed once and for all is somewhat unclear, but an article in the *Hibernian Magazine* in 1783 referred to it in the past tense, noting that there 'formerly stood a pedestrian statue of General Blakeney at the site, but what became of it we know not.'[15] A 1926 article in the *Irish Independent* on this mysterious statue claimed that it was taken to the brass foundry at Clondalkin and melted down to make cannon[16], but this claim does not appear to be repeated elsewhere. It seems that, just like Lord Nelson who came later, the first monument to stand in this location was doomed from the beginning.

British Imperial Monuments in Dublin before Nelson.

As Yvonne Whelan has noted, public monuments are among the most strikingly symbolic features of any town or city, and they play an important role with regards to identity and meaning. Public monuments are 'not merely ornamental features of the urban landscape but rather highly symbolic signifiers that confer meaning on the city and transform neutral places into ideologically charged sites.'[17] In the eighteenth and nineteenth centuries, monuments erected in the city of Dublin would prove divisive, presenting the city as one at the heart of an Empire from which some were seeking to remove the island entirely.

Before the construction of the Nelson Pillar, several monuments to royalty and other figures of British importance were already present in the city. Undoubtedly the most controversial of the pre-existing works in Dublin was the monument to King William of Orange on College Green. The work of Grinling Gibbons, the monument was completed in 1701, only eleven years after the Battle of the Boyne, and within the lifetime of King William of Orange. The statue featured King William III upon a horse, with laurels of victory around his head. As M. G. Sullivan has noted, this statue served a symbolic purpose, and it was clear from the date of its erection that 'the statue was not simply an ornament or a memoir, but was intended as a symbol and constant reminder of Protestant victory over Irish Catholicism.'[18] This statue was frequently the victim of attack, for example in 1710, when its baton was stolen and the statue was smeared with mud. Three students from the nearby Trinity College were fined £1,000 and given a six-month jail sentence for their crimes against the work.[19]

The statue became a site of annual rituals for loyalists in the city. In the early nineteenth century it was common for Orangemen to gather in July and November, dates that marked both the anniversary of the Battle of the Boyne and the birth of the king. The statue would be decorated with orange symbols, and shamrocks would be strewn under the feet of the horse to symbolise his victory over Catholic forces. Even before the erection of the statue, William was celebrated on the streets of Dublin. Jacqueline Hill has noted that 'William's birthday had been celebrated in Dublin as early as 1690, on which occasion a military procession took place, and in the evening the lords justices entertained the leading citizens to dinner.'[20]

The monument to King William III at College Green, from
Ireland in Pictures, 1898.

One beautifully illustrated work on Ireland, published in 1898, produced the image above and a description of Gibbons' statue:

This equestrian statue of William III stands in College Green, and has stood there, more or less, since AD 1701. We say more or less because no statue in the world, perhaps, has been subject to so many vicissitudes. It has been insulted, mutilated and blown up so many times, that the original figure, never particularly graceful, is now a battered wreck, pieced and patched together, like an old, worn out garment.[21]

King George I gazed down on Dubliners from his vantage point on Essex Bridge from 1722, though today this monument can be viewed at the Barber Institute in Birmingham. Its simple inscription reads: 'This statue of George I by John van Nost the Elder was erected in Dublin in 1722 and bought for the Barber Institute in 1937.' This equestrian statue remained on the bridge until 1753, when it was removed owing to the rebuilding of the bridge, known to Dubliners today as the Grattan Bridge. Eventually placed in the grounds of the Mansion House, a new inscription was placed on its pedestal in 1798. Despite the symbolism now associated with that year in Irish history, the new inscription certainly took no pride in Theobald Wolfe Tone or the other revolutionaries, instead noting:

> Be it remembered that at the time when Rebellion and Disloyalty were the characteristics of the day, the Loyal Corporation of the city re-elevated this statue of the First Monarch of the illustrious House of Hanover. Thomas Fleming, Lord Mayor, Jonas Paisley and William Henry Archer, Sheriffs Anno Domini 1798.[22]

1758 would see the placement of another statue to monarchy in the city, with King George II placed within St Stephen's Green, the work of John Van Nost the Younger. Yet another equestrian statue, one commentator in 1818 noted that this statue was also the frequent victim of sabotage and attack:

> Many curious circumstances are connected with this statue: For a number of years it appeared to be destined to fall like that of Sejanus by the hands

of ruffians; from its remote situation, mid-night
depredators were induced to make a trial of their
skill in sawing off a leg or an arm for the value of
the material.[23]

The nineteenth century would see the erection of many
further monuments in the city, commemorating and
celebrating not only figures from the monarchy but also
figures of the British military establishment. Lord Nelson
on Sackville Street was followed by the obelisk to the
Duke of Wellington in the Phoenix Park in 1817, though
it was not completed until the 1860s. The Earl of Eglinton
joined George II in St Stephen's Green from 1866, while
a monument to the Earl of Carlisle was erected in the
Phoenix Park in 1871. Lord Gough would join Wellington
and the Earl of Carlisle there too in 1880, the work of
the celebrated sculptor John Henry Foley, though it was
completed after his passing by the sculptor Thomas Brock.
There were other monuments too, though the above are
among the most familiar to Dubliners. Perhaps that is due
to the fact that, with the exception of Wellington, who
remains standing in the Phoenix Park, all the others were
destroyed by republican bombs, as will be examined in a
later chapter.

2. Nelson and the Ireland of his Time

'*Oh the French are on the sea,' says the Sean Bhean Bhocht,*
'*The French are on the sea,' says the Sean Bhean Bhocht,*
'*Oh The French are in the Bay, they'll be here without delay,*
And the Orange will decay,' says the Sean Bhean Bhocht.[24]

Antique illustration of Horatio Nelson.

O n 2 October 1798, in that year of famed rebellion in Ireland, news of the apparent downfall of Napoleon Bonaparte was greeted by many with wild celebration on the streets of Dublin. As reports of the Battle of the Nile spread throughout the Empire, celebrations were underway at home and abroad, with *The Times* of London proclaiming that 'A victory more glorious or complete is not recorded in the annals of our navy.'[25] In his classic account of the 1798 rebellion, Thomas Pakenham has painted a vivid picture of Dublin at the time as a city that was illuminated and cheerful:

> To cram more candles into their windows, people used potatoes as candlesticks; the streets were crowded, according to the *Evening Post,* with 'groups singing 'God Save the King' and 'Rule Britannia'. Various devices were erected on prominent buildings – an illuminated transparency of George III on the Mansion House, and another on the Post Office of the brave Admiral Nelson defending with his sword the Harp and the Crown. It was months since the Irish loyalists had felt such a glow of patriotism.[26]

The presence of the imagery of Nelson in the celebrations of the Irish capital indicates the extent to which he was viewed as a hero by many in the city, even during a year when the overthrow of British rule in Ireland was the aspiration of a revolutionary minority within the populace. His presence certainly showed that he was a well-known figure in the public mindset.

Who was the man whose image was illuminated in Dublin? Horatio Nelson was born on 29 September 1758, at Burnham Thorpe in Norfolk. He was the sixth child and the fifth son of the Reverend Edmund Nelson, and in the words of his biographer Geoffrey Bennett, he was 'taught the virtues of discipline, and encouraged to stand on his own young feet, in the vigorous and frugal life of a staunch Protestant household.'[27] It was the influence of his uncle, however, Royal Navy officer Maurice Suckling, which brought him to a life in the Navy. Suckling was responsible for Horatio entering the books of the *Raisonnable,* which he commanded, in 1771. While he may have entered the Navy as a young protégé of his uncle, today he is considered one of the quintessential heroes of British history for his involvement with this force, achieving total control of the seas against French and Spanish opposition during the Napoleonic Wars.

A strong mythology has grown up around Nelson, who is remembered for bold action as a commander at sea, often at great personal risk. Nelson lost his right arm as a result of the Battle of Santa Cruz de Tenerife in 1797, and was blinded in one eye earlier in his career, and this sense that Nelson was always willing to risk his own life and limb was part of his public appeal. Indeed, he was something of a public celebrity in British life from the late 1790s. He is most closely associated with the Battle of Trafalgar in 1805, a definitive British victory over the combined French and Spanish fleet, where not a single British vessel was lost, though Nelson personally sustained injuries that cost him his life. Angus Konstam has noted that 'the whole process of celebration, deification and national pride began almost before the smoke of battle had cleared.'[28] His funeral in January 1806 remains one of the most lavish ever witnessed in London, with captured French and Spanish flags adorning the walls of Saint Paul's Cathedral. His place in history was long secured by the time of Trafalgar, not so much for who he was as for what he came to represent to the British public.

To sections of the Irish public, however, France was not an enemy but a potential ally. The outbreak of war between Britain and France in 1793 had a profound effect on the island of Ireland, where revolutionary feelings existed among an active minority of the people, who found inspiration in revolutions farther afield. Ireland was an island that had deep-rooted sectarian divisions among the people, which were coming to the fore, and as David Ryan has observed, 'the shape of Irish society in the eighteenth century was determined by the wars of the seventeenth, when Catholics and Protestants struggled for mastery of the country.'[29] There were restrictions in place against the Presbyterian community in Ireland too, effectively second-class citizens in a society that ensured Protestant rule. Despite the fact that the vast majority of the Irish populace was Catholic, Michael Kenny has noted that 'political and economic power remained firmly in the hands of Protestants, however, and they controlled the army, finance, education and the trade guilds.'[30] While some of the restrictions against Catholics were removed by legislation in the later years of the century, others firmly remained in place. It was out of this divided society that republicanism would emerge in Ireland.

The Society of the United Irishmen had been established in Belfast in 1791, initially as a movement that sought parliamentary reform and further rights for Catholics and Presbyterians. With Catholic, Protestant and Presbyterian men in its ranks, the initial moderate approach of this new movement is evident from its fundamental resolutions, which stated:

1. That the weight of English influence in the government of this country is so great, as to require a cordial union among all the people of Ireland,

to maintain that balance which is essential to the preservation of our liberties and the extension of our commerce. 2. That the sole constitutional mode by which this influence can be opposed, is by a complete and radical reform of the representation of the people in Parliament. 3. That no reform is just which does not include every Irishman of every religious persuasion.[31]

The movement drifted towards more radical politics following its being outlawed upon the outbreak of war with France, and looked more and more to the French Republic, both for political inspiration and military support for any potential revolutionary action in Ireland. In Dublin, the movement had many notable figures in its ranks, such as the Trinity College Dublin graduate Theobald Wolfe Tone, a Protestant champion of the rights of the Catholic majority

Emblem of the United Irish movement. Note the words around the harp: 'Equality – it is new strung and shall be heard'.

in Ireland, who would later be regarded by generations of Irish republicans as the father figure of their ideology. Far from being an inward-looking organisation, R. B. McDowell has noted that the society corresponded with organisations such as the Norwich Revolution Society, the Derby Political Society, the Friends of the People of

London, and others. It also 'displayed its solidarity with British radicalism by electing Thomas Paine to honorary membership.'[32] It met openly for a period in Dublin before it was outlawed, in places like the celebrated Eagle Tavern on Eustace Street, the Music Hall on Fishamble Street and Tailors' Hall.

The United Irish movement would attempt revolution in the late 1790s, seeking military assistance from the French Republic. In 1796, Theobald Wolfe Tone was among a French expedition that made it painfully close to the Irish shore at Bantry Bay, but ultimately failed to land. 'I never saw such dreadful weather',[33] Tone himself would write in the aftermath of this failed landing. Two years later, when the French ultimately did land on the Irish coast at Killala, it was too little and far too late. Under the leadership of General Jean Joseph Amable Humbert, the French arrived to an island where the United Irish movement was in disarray, with many members of its leadership imprisoned or already sentenced to death, and little popular support or appetite remaining for revolution.

What was the role of Horatio Nelson in all of this? Ruán O'Donnell, in his study of Robert Emmet, notes correctly that while Nelson was not personally involved in the interception of French military support to Ireland, his actions elsewhere greatly limited French ability to assist Irish republicans:

> French interest was affected by their limited resources, which were not as plentiful as they had been in 1796–97. Nelson's destruction of Napoleon's Egyptian army transports in Aboukir Bay on 1 August 1798 further strained French capacity to aid Ireland, as did attrition in the Caribbean and Indian Ocean.[34]

An unusual connection exists between Horatio Nelson and the United Irish revolutionaries in the form of Colonel Edward Marcus Despard, an Irish soldier from Queens County (Laois), who lived an extraordinary life. Born in 1751, Despard was educated at the Quaker school in Ballitore, Co. Kildare, and went on to become an ensign in the 50th Regiment of the British Army. Despard was promoted to lieutenant in 1772, and his military career saw him achieve further promotions. James Quinn provides good detail of Despard's military career in his entry for the Dictionary of Irish Biography, noting that:

> In June 1779 Spain declared war on Britain and in January 1780 Despard was appointed chief engineer on an expedition to seize the Spanish fort of San Juan, which commanded access to Lake Nicaragua. He proved himself a skilled engineer and a brave and resourceful soldier, and was popular with his fellow officers, who included Capt. Horatio Nelson, R.N. Nelson and Despard undertook several daring missions together and became good friends. The expedition captured the fort on 29 April 1780, but evacuated it in January 1781. Despard then returned to Jamaica, his reputation one of the few enhanced in an undistinguished campaign.[35]

Despard was appointed superintendent of Honduras in 1784, tasked with overseeing territory Spain had ceded to Britain the previous year. Interestingly, Despard was recalled to London in 1789 because of questions surrounding his conduct. Despard had married a black woman, Catherine, during his time in Honduras, and there was a belief that Despard granted too much in the way of rights to freed slaves. In 1791 he was sued for seizing ten American vessels during his time as superintendent of Honduras, and while awaiting trial he was imprisoned for almost three years.

Quinn has noted that this period of imprisonment had a profound effect on him, as he would emerge 'deeply embittered by his treatment, and turned to political radicalism.'[36] Despard would become active with the United Britons, a movement affiliated to the United Irish movement at home, and in 1802 Despard was arrested for allegedly plotting the assassination of King George III. Just how serious or advanced this plot was remains disputed, but it was claimed that Despard wished to spark a revolution of the masses through his actions. A colourful and dismissive British source from the early nineteenth century claims that, as Despard killed the Monarch:

> At the same moment, other parties were to seize the tower, to surround the two houses of Parliament, to take possession of the bank, to destroy the telegraph, and to stop the mail coaches, which last event was to be, as in the Irish rebellion, a signal for a general rising across the country.[37]

At the trial of this former soldier of Empire turned revolutionary, there was a rather incredible moment when Horatio Nelson rose to speak, giving an account of the character of Despard, a man he admittedly had not seen in many years:

> I formed the highest opinion of him at the time, as a man and as an officer, seeing him so willing in the service of his Sovereign. Having lost sight of him for the last twenty years, if I had been asked my opinion of him, I should certainly have said, if he is still alive he is certainly one of the brightest ornaments of the British Army.[38]

Sadly for Despard, even such a character reference from Horatio Nelson would not spare his life, and like so many United Irishmen at home he was ultimately publicly executed, with a huge crowd gathering at Horsemonger Lane Gaol in 1803 to witness the execution of a one-time friend of Horatio Nelson who had aligned himself with Irish radicals. It is safe to say that Horatio would have had little sympathy with the cause of Ireland. Writing from the Caribbean on the day following Saint Patrick's Day in 1785, Nelson complained in a letter to his 'dear friend' William Locker that:

> Yesterday being Saint Patrick's Day, the Irish colours with thirteen stripes in them were hoisted all over the town. I was engaged to dine with the President but sent an excuse, as he suffered those colours to fly. I mention it only to show the principle of these *vagabonds*.[39]

While 1798 may be spoken of in republican circles as 'The Year of Liberty', more for what it represented than what it actually achieved, its aftermath was more defining than the event itself. The Act of Union in 1800 would bind Ireland and Britain in a parliamentary union and, as R. B. McDowell has noted, it was 'the threat of invasion and rebellion' that convinced Prime Minister William Pitt that such legislation was required. A Union that was seen as being of 'strategic necessity' and 'enacted in a time of crisis',[40] it was none the less an astonishing moment in Irish history when the two Houses on College Green voted for their own abolition. The perception that this unpopular piece of legislation was only passed thanks to corruption remains widespread today, and a well-known poem in the aftermath of the event read:

How did they pass the Union?
By perjury and fraud;
By slaves who sold their land for gold,
As Judas sold his God.[41]

Jonah Barrington, an MP who voted against the Act of Union and who later produced several popular memoirs on life in late-eighteenth-century Ireland, wrote bitterly of the legislation thirty years later, writing 'that disastrous measure, called a "legislative Union", extinguished at one blow, the pride, the prosperity, and the Independence of the Irish Nation.'[42]

The popular narrative has it that the closure of the Irish Parliament and the imposition of a system of direct rule began a process of rapid decline for the 'Second City of the Empire', though it must be noted that Dublin was already a strongly divided city prior to this, something evident from the recollections of Benjamin Franklin quoted earlier, or from the shocking findings of the Revd. James Whitelaw. It was not, as the folk history of the city sometimes has it, that the lights went off overnight and the last wealthy man closed the door behind him, abandoning the city to turn into a slum. Nevertheless, the Act of Union had a profound impact on accelerating the decline of Dublin, and encouraging many of the wealthier inhabitants of the city to abandon it, as well as having a hugely negative impact on the Irish economy, with a provision of the Act ensuring that Ireland was to bear two-seventeenths of the total expenditure of the United Kingdom. Daniel O'Connell, a monument to whom would later be positioned in front of Nelson's on Sackville Street, would later refer to the Act of Union as 'a measure which, carried by such illegal, such unconstitutional means – by the scale, notorious as it was, of all our sacred, our judicial, our political institutions

– never could prosper, but must end in calamity, and recoil upon the authors of such evil.'[43]

Dublin would see a second attempt at revolution in 1803, popularly known as 'Emmet's Rebellion'. Robert Emmet, like those who had gone before him, attempted to drum up French support for an insurrection in Ireland, attempting to convince Napoleon of the merits of backing Irish republicans once more. This dependence on French support was detrimental to the movement in Ireland. Some republicans had long opposed it, such as Jemmy Hope, a radical of the movement from Antrim Presbyterian stock who was active in the 1798 rebellion and the planning of the 1803 attempt. To him, it was an 'underplot' and distraction:

> The appearance of a French fleet in Bantry Bay brought the rich farmers and shopkeepers into the societies, and with them, all the corruption essential to the objects of the British Ministry, to foster rebellion, to possess the power of subduing it, and to carry a Legislative Union.[44]

Nelson had played no personal role in leading the naval opposition to French expeditionary landings to Ireland in the 1790s because his own focus was elsewhere, and there is a certain irony in the fact that many Irishmen fought alongside him. Dennis Kennedy, who has carried out considerable research on the Nelson Pillar, notes in his study that it is estimated 'that one quarter to one third of the sailors who manned Nelson's fleet were from Ireland, including 400 from Dublin.'[45] Theobald Wolfe Tone was deeply aware that impoverished Irishmen were the backbone of the British Navy. Writing an appeal to such men in 1796, he asked of them, rather idealistically, 'what is there to hinder you from immediately seizing on every vessel wherein you sail ... hoisting the Irish flag and steering into the ports of Ireland?'[46]

When news of Nelson's victory at Trafalgar reached Dublin in October 1805, there were similar scenes to those witnessed in the city in 1798, as many citizens sang anthems of loyalism and the *Freeman's Journal* proclaimed that:

> To the people of Ireland it should particularly be a matter of great exultation as part of the plan of operations of that fleet [the French] which has been defeated and shattered was an attack on this country.[47]

While he will forever be associated with the victory of the Battle of Trafalgar, he would also fall in his most celebrated hour. Nelson, who would die at the end of a French musket, was brought home on board his beloved *Victory,* in a cask

Antique postcard depicting the fatal wounding of Nelson.

filled with brandy and later wine to preserve his body. *The Times* proclaimed that his death 'had plunged a whole nation into the deepest grief',[48] and Geoffrey Bennett has noted that at Covent Garden Theatre, 'Rule Britannia' was sung with the following additional verse:

> *Again the loud ton'd trump of fame*
> *Proclaims Britannia rules the main*
> *Whilst sorrow whispers Nelson's name,*
> *And mourns the gallant Victor slain,*
> *Rule, brave Britons, rule the main;*
> *Revenge the God-like Hero slain.*[49]

Whilst Nelson was spoken of adoringly in the British press, many in the Irish press viewed his legacy in a similar manner. The *Dublin Penny Journal*, writing of Nelson some years later, would remark:

> Never were the characters of the hero and the patriot more happily blended than in the person of Lord Nelson, and never were great characters exercised with more brilliant success, or directed to the attainment of more useful ends.[50]

With the death of Nelson came the question of commemoration. Across the Empire, monuments to the memory of Britain's most celebrated naval hero would be erected. Dublin was to prove no exception. Indeed, long before Nelson would gaze down over Londoners, a pillar to his honour would stand in Dublin.

3. *Planning and Executing the Nelson Pillar*

'It will, when completed, be an elegant monument
of national gratitude,
worthy like the country by whom it is reared,
and the hero whose gallant prowess it celebrates.'[51]

T he idea of placing a monument to Horatio Nelson in the city of Dublin first emerged only weeks after news of his passing had reached the capital. At a meeting of the Aldermen of Dublin on 18 November 1805, they agreed on 'the expediency of some speedy and practical measure to compliment the memory of Lord Nelson', with agreement that a statue in the city would form a fitting tribute.[52] A second meeting only days later at the Royal Exchange saw the Lord Mayor, James Vance, and a broad selection of figures from Dublin life assemble with the purpose of planning such a memorial. This meeting was given widespread coverage in the contemporary media, with the *Freeman's Journal* noting that the following motion was carried:

> That it is the opinion of this Meeting, that a
> Monument be erected in the city of Dublin to
> record to future ages the brilliant Victories of the

late Lord Viscount Nelson, and to commemorate the loss the Empire has sustained by his ever to be lamented but glorious death.[53]

At this meeting a decision was reached to open a public subscription, allowing Dubliners to contribute financially towards such a project. A Committee was appointed soon afterwards, with many influential Dubliners in its ranks. The name of Arthur Guinness appears, though this is not the founder of the brewery but rather his son and namesake. Considering that the Guinness founder had been a member of the society that had erected the William Blakeney monument in the centre of Sackville Street a generation earlier, this represented something of a continuation of family involvement in the site. Arthur, like his father, had considerable involvement in public life in Dublin. A director of the Bank of Ireland from 1804, he was a supporter of Catholic emancipation at the turn of the century, while still remaining loyalist in political outlook. Nevertheless, he was on occasion the target of nationalist satire and scorn. Joe Joyce, in his entertaining history of the powerful family, reproduces a piece of satire from the contemporary *Milesian Magazine*, which read:

> *To be sure you did hear*
> *Of the Heresy beer*
> *That was made for to poison the Pope?*
> *To hide the brewer a sin is,*
> *And his name is Arthur Guinness;*
> *For salvation he never can hope.*[54]

Also involved in the Committee were members of the La Touche family, a family of Huguenot origins who had firmly established themselves in banking in the capital. Charles Long, the Chief Secretary to the Lord Lieutenant of Ireland, was also appointed to this Committee, as were several members of the Westminster Parliament. It should be noted that the names of both Catholic and Protestant citizens of Dublin appear. To the business class of Dublin, Nelson would have been held in high regard for reopening trade routes with the crushing of the French at sea.

In April 1806, it was reported by *The Times* that this Committee was appealing to artists, and that they would thankfully receive plans and estimates by May of that same year.[55] The Committee had raised £3,827 by December 1807, but the fundraising efforts continued into the year of 1808. It was reported that at a meeting in December of 1807 the Committee put forward a belief:

> That after maturely considering the several plans and estimates which have been laid before this Committee, they are of the opinion, that any structure worthy of the metropolis of Ireland, and of the illustrious character, whose service it is proposed to commemorate, cannot be raised at a less expense than £6,500.[56]

The symbolic laying of the foundation stone for the pillar was set for 15 February 1808, a date specifically chosen to commemorate the anniversary of one of Nelson's victories, at the Battle of Cape St Vincent in 1797. The Duke of Richmond, then Lord Lieutenant of Ireland, led the ceremony. Below is one contemporary account:

> Yesterday, according to previous notice, his Grace the LORD LIEUTENANT proceeded to lay the

first stone of a monument to the memory of the
Illustrious Nelson.

On this occasion the vast assemblage of persons
of every description, the crowds which thronged
the street, and the beauty, fashion and elegance,
which filled the windows of every house from
Cork-hill to the Rotunda, bore sufficient
testimony of how sincerely the Irish heart beat in
unison with those feelings of grateful admiration
which the Monument about to be erected was
intended to record.[57]

The procession that made its way to the site of the
monument included Cavalry, Yeomen Infantry, sailors,
bands playing 'Rule Britannia', Marine Boys, students
and Fellows of Trinity College Dublin, Aldermen of
the City, the Lord Mayor, various state carriages and
members of the Committee behind the memorial. It
was a steadfast showing of loyalty to the Empire in a city
that only five years earlier had seen attempted revolution
on its streets.

A brass plaque was placed in the foundation stone by
the Lord Lieutenant, with the following inscription:

By the Blessing of Almighty GOD, To commemorate
the Transcendent Heroic Achievements of the Right
Honourable HORATIO LORD VISCOUNT
NELSON, Duke of Bronti, in Siciliy, Vice-Admiral of
the White Squadron of His Majesty's Fleet, Who fell
Gloriously in the Battle off CAPE TRAFALGAR,
on the 21st day of October, 1805; when he obtained
for his Country A VICTORY over the COMBINED
FLEET OF FRANCE AND SPAIN, unparalleled

in Naval History; This first STONE of a Triumphal PILLAR was laid BY HIS GRACE, CHARLES DUKE OF RICHMOND and LENNOX, Lord Lieutenant General and General Governor of Ireland, on the 15th Day of February, in the year of our Lord, 1808, and in the 48th Year of the Reign of our most GRACIOUS SOVEREIGN, GEORGE THE THIRD, in the presence of the Committee, appointed by the Subscribers for erecting this monument.

The winning design for the monument to Nelson came from William Wilkins, a young English architect. Erroneously, Wilkins is often credited as the architect of the pillar.

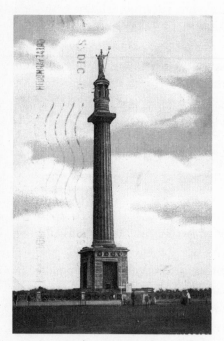

While the Committee viewed Wilkins' design as the finest to enter the competition, they noted their 'regret that the means were not placed in their hands to enable them to gratify him, as well as themselves, by executing his design',[58] and Dublin-based architect Francis Johnston would emerge as the man to lead the project to completion. Several nineteenth-century publications credit Wilkins with the Dublin monument, for

Antique postcard of Wilkins' Nelson memorial at Great Yarmouth.

example, *An Historical Guide to Ancient and Modern Dublin*, published in 1821, which noted that the column 'is after a design of W. Wilkins'.[59] While Wilkins' design was altered significantly, he did design the Nelson memorial at Great Yarmouth in Norfolk, which has many similarities to his original proposal.

Johnston had studied under Thomas Cooley, a distinguished English architect who is remembered today as the architect of the first neo-classical public building in the Irish capital, the Royal Exchange. He has left a lasting architectural legacy to Dublin, and worked on several significant public buildings in the city, such as the Gothic-style Chapel Royal at Dublin Castle, the General Post Office and the Viceregal Lodge in the Phoenix Park, adding both the north and south porticos to what is today the presidential residence.[60] For many years he resided on Eccles Street, and a visitor to 64 Eccles Street today can see the exterior work he himself carried out on what was not his only his residence but his workspace.

Francis Johnson's plans for the pillar would be topped by a Roman eight-oared galley, and would allow a flag to fly from the summit. Indeed, Johnston's own sketch of the pillar showed a Union flag flying from it. The outside of the Nelson Pillar would be constructed of Wicklow granite, while the interior would be comprised of black limestone.

Johnston's column, 134 feet in height, would be complemented by a statue by Thomas Kirk. A Cork-born sculptor, the commission for the thirteen-foot statue of Nelson cemented his place as a rising talent. Kirk's entry in the 1913 *Dictionary of Irish Artists* gives great detail on his family background and early career in Dublin. The son of William Kirk, a native of Edinburgh, Thomas was born in Cork in 1781, but later obtained employment in Dublin with Henry Darley, a stonecutter who employed the young sculptor in 1800. It is noted that 'starting for himself as a sculptor at 21 Jervis Street, he quickly gained recognition as a clever artist and was chosen to execute the colossal figure of Nelson for the memorial column in Sackville Street erected in 1808.'[61] This commission would bring much future work and renown to Kirk, and, as an interesting aside, he even carried out work on a marble bust of Francis Johnston, architect of the pillar. It was first exhibited in 1852, though Kirk himself died in 1845. The Kirk family firmly maintained their family tradition, with the four children of Thomas becoming sculptors in their own right. Joseph Robinson Kirk, the eldest son, was responsible for the four figures upon the campanile of Trinity College Dublin, depicting Medicine, Science, Divinity and Law.

The costs of the pillar were laid out in a pamphlet produced by the Committee, with the following expenditures. The stonecutter's bill was listed at £4,876 11s. 3d. It was noted that the monument contained '22,090 cubic feet black stone, 7,310 cubic feet granite.' Factoring in painting, iron railings, curb and flagging and other costs, the pillar and railing came to £5,587 15s. 8d. in total. When the bill for Thomas Kirk was included, and the cost of the statue, which was listed at £629 2s. 3d. along with a flagstaff, eight lamps, scaffolding and even two flags to fly from the pillar, the ultimate cost of the project was £6,299 18s. 8d.[62] A flag was not to be flown from the monument every single day, but rather to coincide with the anniversaries of Nelson's victories, or with the birthday of a reigning sovereign.

Praise was heaped on the monument in the press, with the *Freeman's Journal* hoping that it would inspire Irishmen to greatness, writing that 'These monuments of national gratitude, while they keep alive in the general bosom the spirit of patriotism, inspire individual valour with the daring impetus of bravery.'[63]

The same newspaper also praised the location of the monument, on the basis that Nelson, a man so closely associated with the seas, was 'within the immediate view of every seaman coming into our port, and cannot fail to gratify the best feelings of that gallant and valuable class of our fellow subjects.'[64]

The memorial to Nelson featured the names and dates of his most celebrated victories. On the south face of the monument the Battle of Trafalgar was marked. The north commemorated the Battle of the Nile. The west side of the monument marked St Vincent, while the east commemorated Copenhagen. 168 steps were all that kept Dubliners from an unrivalled and unparalleled view of their city, from the viewing platform on top of the memorial. Unveiled on the anniversary of the Battle of Trafalgar in 1809, Nelson would quickly become the most controversial monument in the city.

4. *Living with the Nelson Pillar* (1809–1916)

'The Statue of Nelson records the glory of a Mistress and the transformation of our senate into a discount office.'[65]

There were strongly mixed reactions to the pillar from the beginning, unsurprising given the scale of the monument. In the work *History of the City of Dublin: From the Earliest Accounts to the Present Time*, these reactions are discussed in some detail:

> The testimonials of national gratitude and admiration to the memory of this favourite naval hero are already numerous in the British dominions. That erected by public subscription in Dublin is perhaps the greatest of any of them.

Often praised was the inclusion of a viewing platform from the top of the monument, and the same publication noted:

> Within the pedestal and column there are 168 stone steps, to ascend to the top, which has a parapet of iron railing, from whence there is a

NELSON'S PILLAR

Imaginative 1811 illustration depicting the Nelson Pillar
(Image: British Library).

superb panoramic view of the city, the country and
the fine bay.

While the publication may have praised the pillar as the
'greatest' of the existing public monuments to Nelson,
it is clear that they meant this only in terms of its sheer
scale. The publication attacked its 'vast unsightly pedestal',
and went on to claim that while 'it might have a good
effect when viewed at a distance', it 'spoils and blocks up
our finest street, and literally darkens the two other streets
opposite to it.'[66]

Much of the opposition to the Nelson Pillar was not
political initially, but rather concerned with the appearance
of the monument and a belief that it was out of touch and
proportion with the appearance of the street, a judgement
that is reflected in the criticisms above. M. G. Sullivan has
noted that 'the stark, blocky mass of the unadorned base
drew opposition from local residents concerned about the
curtailment of view and circulation',[67] and with Sackville
Street still largely residential, the prying eyes from the top
of the pillar were perhaps not always welcomed by locals.
The nationalistic *Irish Monthly Magazine* took the chance to
attack the monument from a political viewpoint at the time
of the unveiling of Kirk's statue, bemoaning the fact that:

> The statue of Lord Nelson has been placed on the
> column in Sackville Street dedicated to his memory.
> We never remember an exhibition that has excited
> less notice, or was marked with more indifference
> on the part of the Irish public, or at least that part
> who pay the taxes and enjoy none of the plunder.

It went on to decry the pillar further, saying that 'the
statue of Nelson records the glory of a Mistress and the

transformation of our senate into a discount office.'[68] This publication was produced by Watty Cox, formerly the editor of the *Union Star,* a republican newspaper that had accused Arthur Guinness of being a British spy in the 1790s, which was distrusted by some republican figures. One biography of Cox notes that, in relation to the *Irish Monthly Magazine,* 'he carried it on from 1808 to 1815, being subjected to numerous fines and imprisonment for opinions expressed therein.'[69] Certainly, the magazine contained the boldest condemnation of Dublin's new monument.

Unsurprisingly, for loyalists the monument provided a focal meeting point and a place of celebration. In 1809 for example, during a royal jubilee, the pillar was described as being 'splendidly illuminated', as was Dublin Castle. One publication proclaimed that 'the jubilee was marked in this city with a spirit of loyalty and patriotism in the highest

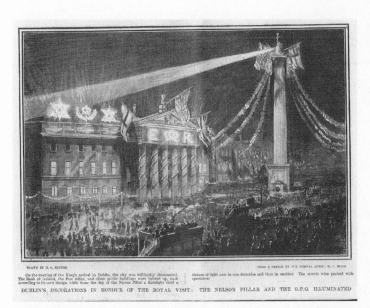

The pillar and General Post Office decorated for a royal visit.

degree honourable to the feelings of the inhabitants.'[70] The pillar continued to be used as a symbol of loyalism, for example in 1863, when fireworks were set off from its viewing platform to mark a royal wedding, a sight that was also common in Dublin during royal visits.

Francis Johnston's pillar was soon joined by his impressive General Post Office, constructed between 1814 and 1818. Only the columns of the facade remain from Johnston's work; the rest was lost to the fires of Easter Week in 1916, which ironically would later make the building become one of the symbols of Irish nationalism. David Dickson has noted that this impressive building, which cost around £50,000, 'marked the final eclipse of Sackville Street as an upper-class residential quarter.' It became the most unusual of things in a city like Dublin: a public building that 'seems to have had no detractors', and it received widespread praise at the time, for example:

> No building in this city has enriched it so much as the General Post Office; independent of its important utility, its erection in Sackville Street has given life and business to the very first of our principal streets, which formerly was nothing more but a mall or Sunday parade for our gentry in winter.[71]

No figure had as profound an impact on early nineteenth-century Ireland as Daniel O'Connell, who came to be seen as the leader of constitutional nationalism. O'Connell was by no means a republican, indeed his ultimate vision for Ireland was the return of Parliament to College Green, and he abhorred violent insurrectionism. There certainly existed a very different image of the man farther afield in his lifetime, with one French republican believing that

O'Connell was a 'gigantic revolutionary … who, with his vigorous arm, is pushing the old world into the depths, and proclaiming the advent of a new right – the right of peoples – and the reign of equality and liberty.'[72] Just what O'Connell, a vocal critic of revolutionary violence in Ireland and France, would have thought of such 'praise' is unclear! Regardless, O'Connell, as a moderate force of change, commanded respect, and could mobilise hundreds of thousands in support of his aims. Frederick Douglass, the great American anti-slavery activist, recalled his time in Dublin in his memoirs, and remembered seeing O'Connell followed through Sackville Street by 'a multitude of little boys and girls', and remembered O'Connell for playfully calling him the 'Black O'Connell of the United States.'[73] O'Connell's movement of reform was a mass movement on an unprecedented scale for Ireland.

The death of Daniel O'Connell during the years of the Famine led to discussions on memorialising him too in the city, with nationalist members of the Corporation

Antique postcard of Daniel O'Connell's monument, showing Nelson behind him.

stating the explicit requirement that any monument to O'Connell would need to be greater than that to Nelson. Reflecting the growing sense of nationalism within Dublin Corporation, one member noted in 1862 that:

> He was the greatest Irishman that ever lived, and, for his part, he would not be content with anything less than a pillar as large as that which commemorates the memory of Nelson. The one earned his fame by slaying his fellow-men, and the other by elevating his countrymen in the social scale, and breaking the fetters by which they were bound without the slaying of blood.[74]

The Dublin monument may have been among the first erected to Nelson in the Empire, but it was by no means the last. Nelson's Column in London was constructed between 1840 and 1843, built to a design by William Railton at a cost of £47,000. It stood taller than the Dublin monument at 170 feet. It too could have fallen victim to militant Irish republicanism in May 1884, when a suspicious package found at the base of the monument was revealed to be made up of dynamite sticks! This attempted attack occurred in the midst of the 'Fenian Dynamite' campaign in Britain, the first co-ordinated bombing campaign of mainland Britain by Irish republicans, which was driven ideologically by the Fenian movement and its Irish-American leadership. On the same day, three bombs did explode in London. It is remarkable that, long before the 1966 explosion in the heart of Dublin, Irish republicans could have done damage to a monument of Horatio Nelson at Trafalgar Square.

Various members of Dublin Corporation voiced displeasure at the location of the Nelson memorial. In 1867 the issue was discussed at length, as the city was

SUPPLEMENT GIVEN AWAY WITH THE WEEKLY FREEMAN   OF AUGUST 19TH 1882 PRICE THREE PENCE.

O'CONNELL MONUMENT — UNVEILED

Contemporary illustration of the unveiling of the O'Connell monument from the *Weekly Freeman*, with Nelson's Pillar clearly visible in the background. Courtesy of the National Library of Ireland.

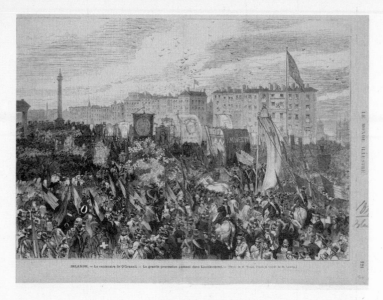

A huge procession in honour of Daniel O'Connell, with the Nelson Pillar visible in the distance. Courtesy of the National Library of Ireland.

debating a location for the memorial to Sir John Gray, which today stands on O'Connell Street. Gray is one of the great overlooked characters of Dublin. A supporter of Daniel O'Connell, he was instrumental in establishing a clean water supply for the city. One Alderman, McSwiney, argued that the location occupied by the pillar should be vacated for a memorial to Gray, insisting that 'the cost of removing the unsightly structure called Nelson's Pillar, which was ruinous to the city, dividing Sackville Street in two, and destroying the vista, would be under £2,000.'[75] The Corporation was largely powerless to move the structure, however, which had been funded by public subscription and was maintained by its own Committee.

Later discussions in the House of Commons also brought the debate of moving the pillar back into public

Antique print by
George Petrie,
showing the pillar
and the General
Post Office in 1830s
Dublin (Image:
British Library).

discourse. An 1891 debate on moving the monument became politically loaded, with two MPs from the north of Ireland the most vocal critics of any attempt to move the Nelson Pillar, leading a Dublin MP to quip that 'those who desire to remove the obstruction are those who view this pillar every day, while those who oppose the removal are gentlemen who are seldom in Dublin at all', while another MP noted: 'It is not a new thing to me to notice that a certain number of persons in the North of Ireland, whose spokesmen are in this House, lose no opportunity of supporting everything that would tend to disfigure the City of Dublin, and of opposing everything that would beautify and improve it.'[76] With debates around the issues of Home Rule and

Irish self-determination, it is easy to see how such a discussion could take a rather political turn.

Some Dubliners learned to take to the pillar. Indeed, in nineteenth- and early twentieth-century newspaper advertisements it is clear that it was used by business premises in the locality to help the curious find their shops – noting that they were near or beside 'Nelson's Pillar' was often enough. Fruit and flower sellers established themselves at the base of the monument, while it also provided a natural location from which city trams could depart. Indeed, the tramway company had petitioned against any attempt to move the pillar in 1891. In many ways, the pillar had become part of the fabric of the city.

Advertisement for Clerys department store, showing the pillar (Image: British Library).

Some modifications were made to the pillar in the 1890s, with an 1894 edition of the *Irish Builder* detailing the new entrance porch to the monument:

The new entrance porch and closing railings have just been carried out, for the trustees, from designs by, and under the superintendence, of Mr. George P. Beater, M.R.I.A.I, architect of this city. The railings are of a massive design, in harmony with the Monument, and add considerably to its appearance. The porch (which, however, is the great feature in the improvements, and which has the name 'NELSON' over the entrance) is of chiselled granite, lined internally with white enamelled brick. Its erection does away with the original and very objectionable approach to the stairs, which are now reached directly from the street level.[77]

With the unusual nature of the pillar and its height in such a low city, there are several instances of arrests for people either climbing the railings or the flagstaff. In 1881, for example, a youngster caused a commotion by 'ascending to the top of the railings' and hopping over, before running around the outside for ten minutes, leading those below to fear he would fall to his death.[78] It was certainly a stupid prank, though there were also tragedies at the pillar. In 1917 an ex-soldier threw himself from the viewing platform to the streets below. Originally from Wolverhampton, and a former soldier with the Royal Field Artillery, the man left a note for his beloved in which he told her 'You are all I have ever loved. Good-bye.'[79] The monument proved central to the celebrations of the centenary of the Battle of Trafalgar in Dublin in October 1905, just as the monument to Nelson in London did, albeit on a much grander scale. The *Irish Independent* proclaimed that 'from the summit of the column hang four large flags, the Royal Standard and the Union Jack being conspicuous features.' The paper also noted that four large wreaths decorated the base of the monument.[80] The steamers being used in the mail service between Holyhead and Kingstown (Dun Laoghaire) were reportedly 'decorated with flags arranged as to show the signalling of the memorable words – England expects that every man will do his duty.'[81] At the Empire Theatre, a bioscope picture of Nelson on screen won lengthy applause from the crowd, who were also treated to a special song written for the occasion by Ralph E. Burnham, entitled 'Lord of the Sea'.[82] The lack of recognition of the centenary from Dublin Corporation was significant, and indicated how municipal politics had changed since the unveiling of the monument almost a century earlier. There was a growing nationalist influence in the Corporation, evident for example in the decision of members to vote against extending a welcome to the visiting King Edward VII in 1903, and this led to political opposition. At the time of the Trafalgar centenary, over 80% of the council members came from a nationalist political outlook.[83]

Nelson had a fine vantage point for the class war of 1913. The Dublin United Transport Company operated routes to and from the pillar, and in late August members of the Irish Transport and

Nelson Pillar, Dublin

Antique postcard of the pillar showing Dublin trams below it.

General Workers' Union, working within this company, and thus employed by its owner William Martin Murphy, took strike action. On 26 August, at the height of the Dublin racing season, Dubliners saw drivers walking away from their trams and pinning the red hand badge of their union to their uniforms. Thousands of workers across various industries in Dublin were 'locked out' by employers in the coming weeks and months, told only to return to work when willing to sign a pledge not to engage with the union any further. On 31 August the Liverpool socialist and trade unionist Jim Larkin addressed a crowd from the window of the Imperial Hotel, directly opposite the General Post Office, and a baton charge on the street below left hundreds injured. An account of this police baton charge, featuring the Nelson Pillar, appeared in a 1914 report into the violence in Dublin:

> The crowd was dispersed by three bodies of police, numbering in all about fifty, who moved out into the street, one from the corner of Lower Abbey Street, another from O'Connell Bridge, and the third from the neighbourhood of the Metropole Hotel. These three bodies of police effectually prevented the crowd from approaching the escort which was guarding Larkin, and turned the crowd back – dispersing them in the direction of the Nelson Pillar and the General Post Office. In the course of the charge by means of which this crowd was dispersed batons were used by many of the police, and a number of civilians were knocked down in the rush back along and across the street, some as the result of blows from batons, and some as the result of collision with and tripping over each other.[84]

Other Dublin Monuments Erected in the Days of the Pillar.

The nineteenth century would see the emergence of a strong nationalist movement in Ireland, embodied by figures like 'The Liberator' Daniel O'Connell and 'The Uncrowned King of Ireland' C. S. Parnell. Constitutional nationalism and the demand for a parliament to sit in Dublin once more would ultimately lead to the Home Rule movement of reform, while more militant Irish nationalists, in the form of republican separatists, were also present in the political spectrum. Both strands of Irish nationalism would seek to honour their dead and their historical lineage in the city, and the nineteenth and early twentieth centuries saw new and very different monuments erected in honour of these men.

On Sackville Street alone, Nelson would be joined by several Irish nationalist figures. The laying of the foundation stone for the O'Connell monument in 1864, and the unveiling of a monument to William Smith O'Brien nearby in 1870, showed the changing political atmosphere in the city clearly. Ian McBride has noted that the laying of the O'Connell foundation stone occurred at a time when he 'was remembered primarily as the successful Liberator of Catholic Ireland rather than the failed Repealer',[85] and huge crowds thronged the Carlisle Bridge, Sackville Street and surrounding streets for the occasion. The Lord Mayor of Dublin spoke, telling the crowd that 'The people of Ireland meet to-day to honour the man whose matchless genius won Emancipation, and whose fearless hand struck off the fetters whereby six million of his countrymen were held in bondage in their own land.'[86] It was not until August 1882 that the figure of O'Connell himself was completed and unveiled, by which point several other Irish nationalists had been honoured with monuments in the city.

The discourse around commemoration was becoming more and more loaded and political, reflecting the political tensions on the island between nationalists and loyalists. When the idea of erecting a statue to Prince Albert on College Green was mooted in 1864, *The Nation* newspaper rallied support against the proposal, and insisted that a statue of Henry Grattan should be placed there instead. 'The idea that Prince Albert's statue would ever be raised in College Green was manifestly as hopeless and wild as a design to move the Hill of Howth', the paper boasted in 1865, when the Albert on College Green idea was well and truly dead in the water.[87] The Grattan statue that still stands on College Green was ultimately erected there instead, on 6 January 1875.

William Smith O'Brien was added to the city landscape in 1870, which was symbolic in that his politics were far more radical than those of constitutional nationalists. O'Brien had been a member of O'Connell's Repeal movement, but he was radicalised in the 1840s, and attempted to lead a rebellion in Tipperary during the course of the famine. Found guilty of high treason, O'Brien was deported to Van Diemen's Land for his revolutionary activities. The erection of a statue to such a figure was a radical departure, and was the first monument to a figure associated with violent resistance to Britain in Ireland.

The opposition of many to the erection of a monument to Prime Minister William Gladstone in the late 1890s was also indicative of a changing political climate in Ireland. In 1898, the Gladstone National Memorial Fund proposed that statues in honour of Gladstone be erected in London, Edinburgh and Dublin. John Hughes was the sculptor chosen for the job at hand. A discussion around acceptance of the statue took place at a meeting of the

Dublin Corporation in August 1898, and ultimately the elected members of the Corporation decided against acceptance of the statue, which infuriated the *Freeman's Journal* newspaper:

> Under the circumstances, it is clear that it is the duty of self-respecting Irishmen to step into the breach, to form a representative committee, to accept the offer of the Duke of Westminster on behalf of the nation, and by the force of public opinion to override the ill-considered and ill-conditioned resolution adopted yesterday. There is no other course open unless Irishmen are to hang their heads in shame for all time at the name of Gladstone.[88]

The actual motion passed by Dublin Corporation is interesting, as it seems that the prime cause of concern to the Corporation was the absence of a statue to Charles Stewart Parnell in the city, with their motion stating 'that no statue should be erected in Dublin in honour of any Englishman until at least the Irish people have raised a fitting monument to the memory of Charles Stewart Parnell.'[89] While Hughes did complete the memorial, it was never placed in Dublin, and instead it now stands in Hawarden in Wales.

While the Corporation may have succeeded in preventing the Gladstone memorial, a monument was erected in February 1908 to Queen Victoria, within the grounds of the Royal Dublin Society at Leinster House. The ceremony saw about 1,000 troops on parade, and a large number of invited guests. The Lord Lieutenant was chosen to unveil the monument, and he noted that 'we are assembled here to dedicate this noble work of art to the perpetual commemoration of a great personality and a great life.'[90] Unsurprisingly, however, this 'noble work of art' became particularly divisive following independence, as Leinster House became the home of the Irish parliament, something that will be examined later in this book.

The monument that was perhaps most relevant to the pillar was that in recognition of Arthur Wellesley, 1st Duke of Wellington. Wellington, though a national British hero like Nelson, had a connection to the city of Dublin as he was born there, and had even served as Irish Chief Secretary. Initially mooted for Merrion Square, where the Duke was born, the Wellington Testimonial was ultimately erected in the Phoenix Park, and only completed in 1861, decades after its foundation stone had been laid. Interestingly, one MP opined, in a letter to the Dublin Wellington Fund, that:

> I quite agree with the Committee in its predilection for a pillar. I was one of the pillarists in the Nelson case and my own wish for our column is to be one of more magnificent dimensions. Great height is the cheapest way and one of the most certain ways of obtaining sublimity.[91]

By October 1911, with the placement of the Charles Stewart Parnell monument at the far end of Sackville Street, Nelson found himself caught between several figures of huge importance to the nationalist community. The Parnell monument was unveiled by John Redmond before a huge gathering. One American newspaper proclaimed that 'the scenes of enthusiasm were only paralleled by those which attended the unveiling of the O'Connell statue at the opposite end of the street thirty years ago',[92] while at home it was believed that 'the occasion was one that must live for all time in the annals not only in Dublin, but in the records that are concerned with the history of the Irish people all the world over.'[93]

Antique print showing a busy Sackville Street in the 1870s. Notice the exaggerated size of the pillar.

5. *Nelson and Easter Week*

'Emmet's two-hour insurrection is nothing to this! They will talk of Dublin in future as one of the splendid cities like they speak to-day of Paris! Dublin's name will be glorious forever.'
– Patrick Pearse inside the General Post Office.[94]

On 24 April 1916, an Irish Republic was proclaimed before the world once more. The Irish Citizen Army,

Postcard depicting destruction around the
pillar after the 1916 rebellion.

which had emerged from the labour disturbances of three years earlier, and the Irish Volunteers, a nationalist separatist movement, were the chief players in this drama on the streets of the capital. Francis Johnston's General Post Office was seized in the frenzy, capturing both customers and staff by surprise, while other buildings on both sides of the Liffey were occupied by revolutionaries.

All over the city, whether at Stephen's Green or Sackville Street, Dubliners and visitors watched an attempt at revolution unfold before their eyes. Nelson had perhaps the finest view in the city. On the steps of the General Post Office the poet, school principal and Irish-language activist Patrick Pearse read a proclamation to a largely bemused crowd of Dubliners, which proclaimed that 'the ownership of Ireland belongs to the people of Ireland.' Across the street, a copy of the proclamation was placed at the foot of the Nelson Pillar, with a stone in each corner.[95] To a young Michael Collins, inside the General Post Office, the rebellion 'had the air of a Greek tragedy about it.'[96] To Pearse, however, the highly symbolic stand redeemed Dublin from the shame of what he termed 'Emmet's two-hour insurrection' in the lifetime of Nelson, and maintained a historic tradition of armed dissent against British rule in Ireland.

The 1916 Proclamation, a copy of which was placed at the Nelson Pillar.

When the first shots rang out on Sackville Street, it became clear to many in the vicinity that this was not a trial run, or revolutionary posturing, as Dubliners accustomed to watching armed men drill in Dublin presumed at first. Sean T. O'Kelly, a later President of Ireland, recalled the arrival of Lancers onto Sackville Street soon after the raising of the flag of the new Irish Republic over the GPO in his statement to the Bureau of Military History:

> I remember hearing some noise as of shouting or cheers in the distance away up towards Parnell Square and some others and I rushed out of the Post Office to the front of the building in O'Connell Street. I arrived just in time to see a number of the Lancers charging down O'Connell Street and fired on from the Post Office building.[97]

As the men approached the pillar, shots rang out from the occupied building, leaving dead men and horses on the streets. With three dead, and one fatally wounded, the first dramatic exchange of the week on Sackville Street occurred right by the pillar. Ernie O'Malley, in his memoirs of the revolutionary period in Ireland, recalled passing the pillar and seeing the morbid spectacle of the remains of dead horses, as well as observing the copy of the Proclamation that lay at the base of this symbol of the British Empire. 'Some looked at it with serious faces, others laughed and sniggered', he recalled. Seated on one of the dead horses just beyond Nelson was a woman, a shawl around her head, drunk and singing a song wishing 'the best of jolly good luck' to the young boys in khaki and blue.[98] A story has entered the folklore of the Easter rebellion that the rebels made an attempt to blow up the monument of Nelson, seeing it as a symbol of British domination in the heart of the city. The story is well recounted in the *Sinn Féin Rebellion Handbook* produced in the aftermath of the insurrection, but was denied by many rebel participants:

> One of the many daring schemes of the rebels which failed was an attempt to blow up the Nelson Pillar in Sackville Street. An eyewitness of the effort stated that he was proceeding to the south side of the city from the north on Tuesday morning, 25th April, at 7 a.m. On reaching the foot of Rutland square he saw an armed rebel driving the spectators up Sackville Street and into Great Britain Street. At this corner the crowd lingered, and the rebel ordered the people to 'get out of the firing line', and added with a dramatic whirl of his bayonet, 'the Nelson Pillar is about to be blown up with bombs.'

The source claims that just after 7 a.m. on the Tuesday morning there was a loud explosion, followed by a cloud of smoke, but:

> The monument, however, did not show any signs of collapse, and although this explosion was followed by three others within ten minutes, the Pillar did not even quiver. No further efforts were then made at the destruction of the monument, and at 7.30 the spectators were again permitted to pass by the Pillar.[99]

This so-called attempt on the pillar has its origins in another story entirely, relating to the issue of home-made grenades and the General Post Office. W. J. Brennan Whitmore, a participant in the Easter rebellion, claimed years later that statues and monuments were the last thing on the minds of the men in the fight. In *Agony at Easter*, a tale is recounted of Lieutenant Liam Clarke of the Irish Volunteers holding a hand-made grenade, which then almost exploded in his face. Luckily, Clarke survived any serious injury, but in the aftermath of the incident men began to test a number of the remaining canisters against the base of the pillar. 'The foundation did not even tremble, nor was the stone chipped', but a rumour did spread at least.[100] They may not have blown up Nelson, but *The Irish Times* did claim that republicans dented the man himself, as 'the figure, and the shaft of the Pillar, are now thickly studded with bullet marks, and one unlucky shot took away the warrior's nose.'[101]

Ironically, while Nelson was not blown up by republicans, he was used by them for protection. Sean McEntee recalled watching two young Volunteers attempt to sprint the gauntlet of O'Connell Street under enemy fire, and watched in awe and horror as:

> On the brave fellows came, their heads bent down, sprinting along a zig-zag course to mar the enemy's aim. Into the cover of Nelson Pillar they ran, and out of it again, upon the second half of their journey.[102]

On the Wednesday of Easter Week, the gunboat Helga sailed up the River Liffey, to be tied up near to the Custom House. From this vantage point, and over the Loopline Bridge, she fired on Liberty Hall, the General Post Office and other sites where it was believed that rebels were located. She did immense damage to Sackville Street, though Nelson avoided a direct hit.

As Nelson, hero of the seas in the eyes of the British public, gazed down over the General Post Office during the week, one of the more bizarre moments of the

Postcard
depicting
destruction to
the General
Post Office
from the
Nelson Pillar.

rebellion occurred when two seamen arrived at the doors
of the building. Liam Tannam of the Irish Volunteers
recounted a story many years later for the Bureau of
Military History:

> ... there were two strange looking men outside and
> I went to the window and I saw two obviously
> foreign men. Judging by the appearance of their
> faces I took them to be seamen. I asked what they
> wanted. The smaller of the two spoke. He said:
> 'I am from Sweden, my friend from Finland. We

want to fight. May we come in?' I asked him why a Swede and Finn would want to fight against the British. I asked him how he had arrived. He said he had come in on a ship, they were part of a crew, that his friend, the Finn, had no English and that he would explain.

So I said: 'Tell me why you want to come in here and fight against England.' He said: 'Finland, a small country, Russia eat her up.' Then he said: 'Sweden, another small country, Russia eat her up too.' 'Russia with the British, therefore, we against.' I said: 'Can you fight? Do you know how to use a weapon?' He said: 'I can use a rifle. My friend – no. He can use what you shoot fowl with.' I said: 'A shotgun.' I decided to admit them. I took them in and got the Swede a rifle, the Finn a shotgun. I put them at my own windows.[103]

Joseph McDonagh, who had participated in the rebellion but avoided arrest, remembered walking the streets of the shattered capital on the day following the surrender of the republican forces. The fires of looters, the endless fighting and the gunboat Helga had flattened much of Sackville Street, and he recalled:

The following day I made my way down to O'Connell St. together with large numbers of the population who were out viewing the ruins of the G.P.O. and the whole of O'Connell St. which I found in ruins. The only object I saw standing, I am sorry to say, was Nelson's Pillar as it is today.[104]

Widespread destruction in the Henry Street area following the rebellion. The side of the General Post Office and the Nelson Pillar are visible. Courtesy of the National Library of Ireland.

Ina Heron, daughter of the Edinburgh socialist and trade unionist James Connolly, executed for his role in the rebellion, recalled her father showing her the monument as a child:

> At Nelson Pillar we were told to take a good look at that statue as it would remain put many years after we had all passed away and would be no more. 'It is a landmark. If in doubt of your direction ask for the Pillar and start off from here. Then you will be making some use of a terrible eyesore.'[105]

As word of the Dublin insurrection spread across the world, the line between fact and fiction became very thin indeed. One New York newspaper claimed that not alone were the bodies of two German military leaders found in Dublin, but that the Nelson Pillar was 'razed' and destroyed in the firefight. They quoted an eyewitness who spoke of the monument in the past tense, noting that 'Nelson's Pillar, opposite the post office, which was hollow and had stairs leading to the top', had been lost to the destruction of the street.[106]

The pillar has made its way into several fictional accounts of the Easter Rising, including Sean O'Casey's celebrated 1926 play *The Plough and the Stars,* with Mrs Gogan frantically informing people 'that the Tommies is sthretched in heaps around Nelson's Pillar an' th' Parnell statue, an' that th' pavin' sets in O'Connell Street is nearly covered be pools o'blood.'[107]

Roddy Doyle includes Nelson in his work, *A Star Called Henry*, a fictional account of Easter Week written by a volunteer of the trade union militia, the Irish Citizen Army. Referred to as the 'one-armed bollocks', in a moment of boredom Nelson is fired upon from the rebels in the General Post Office. 'Got him in the other eye, the hoor. Now lads, back to work.'[108]

Trams return to the city streets following the insurrection, but Sackville Street is reduced to ruins in places. Courtesy of the National Library of Ireland.

6. Gazing Over a Free Ireland.

'That one-armed, one-eyed Admiral of the British bollock-shop institution the Royal Navy has no business on his perch at all. He has no fucking place in Ireland's history but a wrong one.'

– Brendan Behan, in discussion with Rae Jeffs.[109]

An image snapped by legendary photographer W. D. Hogan, showing a crowd from the top of the pillar in Civil War days. Courtesy of the National Library of Ireland.

Nelson survived Easter Week, though much around him did not. Dublin landmarks around him like the Metropole Hotel and the Dublin Bread Company building were totally destroyed, and Francis Johnston's General Post Office was entirely gutted by fire. The rebellion was followed by an intense guerrilla conflict of opposition to British rule in Ireland, and the rise of a political voice of the masses in the form of Sinn Féin, who made huge electoral gains in the 1918 election, in part owing to the decision of Labour to step aside and not contest seats, but also in part due to the mislabelling of the insurrection as the 'Sinn Féin Rebellion'. The foundation of an Irish Free State in 1922 would bring a new elite to power in Ireland, with former revolutionaries in many cases stepping into the clothes of politicians.

Nelson would witness violence once more in 1922, with the Battle of Dublin raging around the pillar. Ireland, like so many post-revolutionary societies, had descended into civil war, with men divided on the issue of accepting a limited form of self-determination from the British Empire. Armoured cars were once more on the streets of the capital, though now driven by Irishmen, and *The Irish Times* reported on the scenes on 3 July 1922 when pro-Treaty forces moved in on republicans holed up on Sackville Street:

> One armoured car took up its position just outside the Metropole, another at the corner of Talbot Street, and a third on the other side of Nelson's Pillar. From here they poured in a rapid fire on the positions ... with machine guns and rifle grenades.[110]

The pillar was used by Free State soldiers during the course of the violence, and a sniper-fire duel between a

Free State soldier at the Nelson Pillar and a republican in the Hamman Hotel ensued on the following day.[111] By the end of the fighting in Dublin, O'Connell Street was once more in ruins, and there were other consequences to the violence. At the Four Courts, the Irish Public Records Office and its priceless historic files were lost to the bombardment of that building by Free State forces. Images printed in Irish and international newspapers showed Dubliners picking up priceless archival materials as far away as the base of the pillar.

When the violence of the Civil War receded, serious discussion opened up regarding the fate of Nelson, as well as other imperial statues and landmarks in the city. Nelson's location, in the very heart of the city opposite what had become a deeply symbolic building, ensured that he would be particularly controversial. The Wellington testimonial in the Phoenix Park, beyond the city, proved much less controversial, and became something of a focal point for Remembrance Sunday ceremonies. In 1926, for example, tens of thousands of ex-servicemen and their families gathered at the Wellington testimonial to attend Remembrance Sunday events. *The Irish Times* reported that:

> It would be hard, indeed, to estimate the size of the gathering. It did not, however, number less than forty thousand. From an early hour people began to arrive by every kind of vehicle and on foot, and an hour before the ceremony began the wide open space in the Phoenix Park surrounding the Wellington Monument was densely crowded.[112]

In February 1922, a month on from independence, an American publisher by the name of Sylvia Beach published

1952 image of the pillar, from the collection of shots of locations relevant to 1916 Rising. Courtesy of Military Archives.

a work by the Dublin author James Joyce in Paris. Titled *Ulysses*, the celebrated work chronicled a single day in the life of Leopold Bloom, a Dublin Jew who moves throughout the city, encountering familiar places and characters, on 16 June 1904. It is unsurprising that Joyce includes the pillar in this work, given the incredible level of detail towards the city within its pages. In it, the character Stephen Dedalus refers to Horatio Nelson as 'the one-handled adulterer', a playful reference to Nelson's well-documented private life. Indeed, Joyce allowed the monument to Horatio Nelson to play quite a prominent role in Episode 7 of his work. Two elderly women ascend the pillar, eating plums and spitting the seeds down on those unfortunate enough to be below them. They 'waddle slowly up the winding staircase', before gazing over the city and 'spitting the plumstones slowly out between the railings.'[113] *Ulysses* also contains an allusion to Nelson in the words of Buck Mulligan, who parodies the famous signal of Nelson at the Battle of Trafalgar. 'Ireland expects that every man this day will do his duty' is a parody on Nelson's signal on the eve of battle, when the *Victory* sent the message that 'England expects that every man will do his duty' to his fleet.[114]

1952 image of the pillar, from the collection of shots of locations relevant to 1916 Rising. Courtesy of Military Archives.

1925 saw major discussion on the pillar and its location. The Dublin Borough Commissioners proposed Nelson's removal, not on political grounds but rather owing to it being 'an obstruction' and interfering with the flow of traffic on O'Connell Street. *The Irish Times* reported that:

> One enterprising Liverpool firm, taking time by the forelock, actually sent a representative across to Dublin to examine the structure and report as to the work that would be entailed in its removal from the present site. The result is that the firm has

made an offer to the Commissioners to take down the Pillar at a cost of £1,000.[115]

In a piece of correspondence now contained in the archives of the Department of the Taoiseach from 1925, the trustees of the pillar suggested that they were willing to consider the removal of the pillar if it would be re-erected elsewhere. In a letter from the Town Clerk to the office of the Taoiseach it was claimed that 'one of the suggestions is the Phoenix Park, as a companion monument to the Wellington Column.' The Wellington monument would have dwarfed Nelson, however, being of a far larger scale.[116] In the same year, Howth Urban District Council expressed an interest in acquiring the pillar, should it be dismantled, and re-erecting it on the Hill of Howth. By October, the newspapers were claiming that Nelson

Valentine collection showing the view offered by the pillar, facing towards Westmoreland Street and D'Olier Street. Courtesy of the National Library of Ireland.

was set to go, but some architects rushed to its defence. Architect Manning Robertson proclaimed that the pillar was 'the one monument in the city he would be proud to bring a foreign architect to see',[117] but he and others need not have feared for its imminent removal as the Commissioners were in fact quite powerless to remove it without an Act of the Oireachtas. Nevertheless, the issue would re-emerge endlessly over the following years, with Dublin Corporation calling on the City Manager to approach the government with the idea of removing the monument in 1931. At a rather heated meeting, Jim Larkin denounced the monument and Nelson, stating that 'the pillar had been erected despite the people and Dublin', and that 'although Nelson might have some historical value to other nations, he had none for Ireland.'[118]

The pillar was discussed in the Dáil and the Seanad on several occasions in the years following independence. Sean MacEntee stated in the Dáil in 1949 that, by allowing the pillar to remain standing in an independent Ireland, 'we did not honour Nelson. We allowed him to remain there, as I have said, to remind our people of what they had suffered and what they had overcome.'[119] William Butler Yeats, a Senator in the Irish Free State, made a very interesting intervention in the debate on the subject in 1923, which is often misrepresented. Yeats did favour the removal of the pillar, but believed that, if possible, it should be erected in another location because of its historic significance to a minority of the population:

> I can see that it is an obstruction from a civic point of view, but I am primarily interested in the matter from an aesthetic point of view. Nelson's Pillar divides that long street into two. I think it

would be much better to display the length of the street. The more sense of space we can get there the better, we should make the most of the vista. Then Nelson's Pillar dwarfs the Parnell monument, which, without being very interesting, is a finer monument. But if another suitable site can be found Nelson's Pillar should not be broken up. It represents the feeling of Protestant Ireland for a man who helped to break the power of Napoleon. The life and work of the people who built it are part of our tradition. I think we should accept the whole part of this nation and not pick and choose. However it is not a beautiful object.[120]

The pillar was challenged in the 1930s by the Blueshirt movement, who had emerged from the Army Comrades' Association. Led by former Garda Commissioner Eoin O'Duffy, the Blueshirts would later fight in Spain in opposition to the Spanish Republic and in support of General Franco's fascist coup. In a 1935 edition of *The Blueshirt* newspaper, the front page bemoaned the fact that:

> O'Connell Street, the main thoroughfare of Dublin, is the only street in our capital which makes any show of statues to Irish patriots. Yet even there O'Connell and all the rest are dominated by a monument to an English sailor who never earned, morally or in any other way, the slightest claim to Irish respect or gratitude.
>
> When Irishmen cease to be irritated at the sight of Nelson dominating O'Connell Street, or Victoria squatting at the front door of Leinster House, the

national spirit is indeed in a bad way. The conqueror is gone, but the scars which he left still remain and the victim will not even try to remove them.[121]

P. S. O'Hegarty, the prominent writer and historian, outlined his belief in a letter to the *Evening Herald* in December 1931 that 'Nelson, and Queen Victoria, and other British statues are ancient monuments, trophies left behind by a civilisation which has lost the eight centuries' battle. The hand that touches one of them is the hand of an ignoramus and a vandal.'[122]

The 1930s saw several campaigns emerge with the unusual aim of retaining the column of the pillar while replacing the controversial figure on top of it. This approach took into account the popularity of the viewing platform and the structure among Dubliners, while acknowledging the controversial nature of the statue itself. In 1931, a letter written to *The Irish Times* highlighted the statue of the Virgin Mary within the Carmelite Church on Whitefriar Street. This celebrated statue pre-dates the reformation, and had apparently survived the days of anti-Catholic sectarianism by being hidden by worshippers. Dublin folklore suggests that it found a brief life hollowed out and buried face down as a pig trough. Although there is no hard evidence to support this claim, it was actually rather common for statues of its time to be hollowed out. The writer asked:

> Would not a replica of this figure be a suitable crown to that noble piece of architecture which all agree the Pillar itself is? The citizens of Dublin, visitors from all parts of the world, the young and hopeful, the old, the weary and heavy-laden, could not fail to find comfort and hope in the contemplation of

a figure representing her chosen by God for his purposes towards mankind.[123]

Far removed from the writer of that letter, Clare County Council passed a motion seeking to put the Protestant republican Theobald Wolfe Tone on top of the pillar in 1937, noting that 'the figure of a British admiral' should come down, to be replaced by 'a figure of the father of Irish republicanism.'[124] A few decades later, Saint Patrick was proposed in 1961, which led Myles na Copaleen (the journalistic alias of Brian O'Nolan, or Flann O'Brien) to quip that:

> Defeat of the French should endear Nelson to all clear-thinking Irishmen. Today, the French are the most decadent nation in Europe, possibly in the world. Although they share all the conventional diseases of civilised man, no other ethnic group on the face of the earth can match their alcoholism. Millions of them walk around demented, and half a million are in fact locked up.[125]

The archives of the Department of An Taoiseach contain letters from all across Ireland in the decades that followed independence, proposing suitable replacements, or the removal of the monument outright. One of the more interesting letters comes from 1956, sent by a Fianna Fáil Club in rural Ireland, and written by hand. It called for 'the young and noble Protestant' Robert Emmet to take the finest vantage point over Dublin, in the hope that 'it may inspire the young Protestants of the North to claim Ireland as their own.'[126] In the same year, the 'Federation of the I.R.A 1916–1931' wrote to the Taoiseach complaining that the pillar constituted a 'national affront' to the people of Ireland,

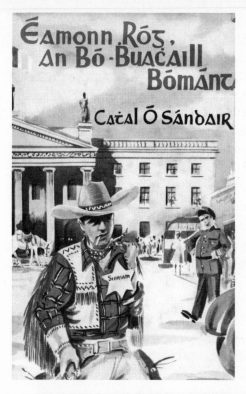

Éamonn Rós,
An Bó-Buacaill
Bómánc
Catal Ó Sándair

A very unusual 1960 book cover for a work by Cathal Ó Sándair featuring the pillar. With thanks to Cathal's family and HiTone blog.

seeking its immediate removal.[127]

Proposals for the replacement of Nelson did not always come from home. One suggestion came from a radical trade unionist in the United States, known as Red Mike Quill. Originally from Kerry, Quill was one of the most feared and respected trade union leaders in America, and helped to establish the Transport Workers' Union of America.

Quill took an active role in the Irish Civil War, opposing the Anglo-Irish Treaty and participating in the capture of Kenmare by republican forces. In a 2002 address at a SIPTU conference in Kerry, Manus O'Riordan stated that 'during those years Mike Quill also had his first experience of industrial struggle when he and his brother John were fired for staging a sit-in strike in a Kenmare saw-mill.'[128]

Like many men who had fought in the Civil War, Quill was to settle in the United States, arriving in 1926. Quill found himself employed with the Interborough Rapid Transit Company (IRT), having first worked in a variety of jobs. The IRT was the private operator of the New York underground of the day, and Quill was among the men to bring the Transport Workers' Union of America into existence in April 1934. Quill would go on to become one of the most influential and capable union leaders of his time, organising men who worked on the New York underground. The name of the union was inspired by the Irish Transport and General Workers' Union, the vehicle of Jim Larkin and James Connolly.

Many of the workers around the new union were Irish migrants, and indeed many, like Quill, had been veterans of the revolutionary period. As historian Brian Hanley has noted:

> It was a combination of former IRA veterans, among them Quill and Gerald O'Reilly, members of the Clan na Gael, activists in the Communist Irish Workers Clubs and the American Communist Party itself which proved crucial to the foundation of the TWU.[129]

In January 1964, Quill made the offer on behalf of the Transport Workers' Union 'cheerfully to finance the removal of Lord Nelson.' He made this unexpected offer in a letter to the city authorities, and it was responded to publicly by Sean Moore, then Lord Mayor of Dublin. *The Irish Times* reported the Lord Mayor as stating that the Corporation had no power to remove Nelson, as the monument was under the guardianship of trustees.

The Irish Times noted that Quill said that his union would pay for the removal of Nelson from his pedestal and his transportation to Buckingham Palace, where he said

Nelson was 'respected and loved for his many and victorious gallant battles on behalf of the British Crown.' Quill wrote that he believed that the statue gave the impression to visitors, owing to its sheer scale, that to the Irish it meant what the Statue of Liberty meant to Americans. Quill suggested a statue of Patrick Pearse, James Connolly or Jim Larkin be placed on top of the pillar instead of Nelson. As a compromise, 'since there are two governments in Ireland today', Quill suggested President John F. Kennedy as a statue to place in the centre of O'Connell Street. Kennedy had been assassinated only months earlier in November 1963, and discussions were under way regarding a potential monument for Kennedy in Ireland.

Quill noted that his union was willing to finance the removal of Admiral Nelson 'in a dignified manner and without hatred or rancour on the part of anybody.' The Lord Mayor of Dublin thanked Quill for his offer. The newspaper noted, though, that it never came to pass.[130]

There was also talk of moving Nelson to Northern Ireland, where he might be more appreciated. The Prime Minister of the six counties was reported in the *Irish Independent* in 1955 as stating that there was no desire to erect the statue in Belfast, though one northern politician did suggest to him that 'Northern Ireland send a statue of William on a white horse in exchange for Nelson.'[131]

Guidebooks to the city of Dublin in the decades after independence give a good idea of the perception of the pillar, and Dubliners' attitudes to it. One 1940s guidebook on the city made the argument, that while Nelson was out of touch with the narrative of the new State:

> Many people wonder why he is allowed to remain there, now that Ireland is free, but the general feeling is that the cost of taking down the Pillar

Looking down over Dublin, a snapshot from the top in 1942.
With thanks to Jacolette.

would be out of all proportion to the kick the
Dubliners would get out of it, and so it remains.[132]

John Harvey's brilliant 1949 guide to Dublin, which was
praised by George Bernard Shaw, attacked those who
argued for its removal, noting:

> The Nelson Pillar is a grand work, without which
> the long stretch of O'Connell Street would lose
> much of its vitality. Fatuous suggestions for its
> removal have come from traffic maniacs who,
> apart from their total disregard for aesthetics, fail
> to visualise the chaos which would result from
> creating a through current of cross-town traffic at
> this point.[133]

Chiang Lee, a Chinese visitor, recalled a trip to the top of
the pillar in *The Silent Traveller in Ireland,* published in the
early 1950s. Lee recalled that visitors from all over could be

found at the pillar, and 'I had not realised that Dublin was so very cosmopolitan. Several foreign languages were being spoken, but there were a great many more Irish people than tourists.'[134] Among the languages Lee heard at the pillar was our native language, totally new and alien to the visiting writer. These men refused to speak in English, and were identifiable by their small metal rings. The irony in locals refusing to address a visitor in the English language, presumably on nationalist grounds, while enjoying the view from the top of a monument to a British naval hero, is something Lee didn't pick up on.

One of the most spirited defences of the pillar ever made came from Thomas Bodkin, who discussed the monument at length on Irish radio in 1955. Bodkin was a senior and respected voice in the world of art and culture, who had served as Director of the National Gallery of Ireland from 1927 to 1935. In his defence of the monument, he noted that:

> People talk about Nelson in a way I can't stomach. He is described as a one-eyed monster or a one-armed adulterer by some present-day Dublin citizens. The fact is he was a man of extraordinary gallantry. He lost his eye fighting bravely, and his arm in similar fashion.

Bodkin went on to state that 'Man and boy I have lived in Dublin, off and on, for 68 years. When I was a young fellow we didn't talk about Nelson's Column or Nelson's Pillar, we spoke of the Pillar, and everyone knew what we meant.'[135] This feeling, that the pillar and the man above it were separate, is common among Dubliners even today. To Bodkin and others, the pillar was first and foremost an opportunity to view Dublin from a new and exciting angle.

Just as Joyce had, a new generation of Irish writers continued to engage with the unavoidable monument. Brendan Behan, for example, wrote of it in *Confessions of an Irish Rebel,* where he had little good to say of it. To him, 'the oldest Dubliners, the descendants of the native Irish that crept in and settled around Ballybough (an Baile Bocht, the poor town) regarded the Wellington Monument and Nelson's Pillar as a gibe at their own helplessness in their own country.'[136] We know the views of a young Brendan Behan on both Wellington and Nelson rather well too. While imprisoned in the British Borstal system for his republican activities in 1940, the possibility of early discharge for Brendan was discussed by authorities. Michael O'Sullivan, in his study of Brendan Behan's life and times, quotes an entry on his Borstal file dated 20 December 1940, which noted:

> He wants to be expelled to Ireland for all his relations are there. He feels that the expulsion order will clarify the position and help him. He would go to sea if this were insisted upon, but he says he is always sea-sick, and being a good Irishman, he has a good deal of respect for Wellington but none at all for Nelson![137]

In poetry, the pillar appears in the work of Austin Clarke, within his collection *Too Great a Vine.* Clarke argued against the removal of the pillar, writing:

> *No, let him watch the sky*
> *With those who rule. Stone eye*
> *And telescopes can prove*
> *Our blessings are above ...*[138]

Perhaps most famously, northern poet Louis MacNeice placed the monument in his poem 'Dublin', a tribute to a city that he was not born in, but felt a great affinity towards. To MacNeice, Nelson was standing over a new Ireland where everything had changed, 'watching his world collapse.' Prophetic words, which were later adopted by The Dubliners folk band for their hit single 'Nelson's Farewell'.

To some Dubliners, as the decades wore on, Nelson had won a sort of squatters' rights claim to O'Connell Street. Others, like Brendan Behan, could only see a monument of colonialism. If Nelson's future was debated, it was not the only monument of its kind in the city.

7. Contested Iconography in an Independent Ireland

'The sooner we go ahead with the job of removing every symbol of British rule in Ireland, the sooner we can make Ireland, in fact, what she is of right – queen of her own affairs.'

– National Student Council spokesperson,
November 1955.[139]

Following the achievement of limited Irish independence in 1922, many monuments in the Irish capital erected during the time of British rule in Ireland would be removed by official or unofficial means. In some cases the decision was made by authorities to remove monuments and symbols from the streets of the capital, though in many more cases it was the actions of republicans that would alter the streetscape of Dublin. Incredibly, many of the bombings carried out against monuments and statues in the city were not officially endorsed by the IRA leadership, but were rather the actions of splinter groups or individuals.

One of the first monuments in Ireland to fall victim to attack was actually outside of the capital: the monument to Lord Dunkellin in Galway. An Anglo-Irish soldier and politician, Dunkellin had fought in the Crimean War and was an elected Member of Parliament for Galway Borough from the 1850s. In May 1922, a huge crowd in Galway proceeded to attack Dunkellin's monument at Eyre Square, toppling it and leading the *Galway Observer* to note:

> On Thursday night a crowd numbering several thousand assembled inside the Square, and two men set to work sawing at the base of the life-size bronze monument of Lord Dunkellin, a brother of the late Lord Clanricarde. A rope was afterwards procured and fastened around the neck and, with a strong pull, over it went amidst great applause.

This act of defiance was spearheaded by local trade union leaders, who informed the crowd that the statue 'was a symbol of landlord tyranny, and they intended to pull down every symbol of its kind in Ireland and put a monument of some good Irishman in its place.' The crowd marched through the streets of Galway with the toppled statue, before ultimately throwing it off a pier. The *Observer* finished its report on proceedings by noting that, 'As the body was hurried into the sea, the band amidst a roar of joyous laughter, played "I'm forever blowing bubbles".'[140]

Armistice Day in Dublin in 1928 saw an attack carried out on the statue of King William III at College Green, as well as an attempt on the statue of King George II in St Stephen's Green. Armistice Day had seen very significant clashes between republicans and those marking the day of commemoration right throughout the decade, with the British Legion's decision to open an office in the capital in 1925 in particular attracting the scorn of republicans, and the attacks of Armistice Day in 1928 must be seen in the context of that opposition. *The Irish Times* reported on 12 November 1928 that republicans had left what was believed to be a landmine at the William statue, leading to 'a tremendous explosion', which ultimately did more damage to neighbouring property than to the monument itself. Shortly afterwards, an explosion at the Green did minor damage to the statue of George II. On the very same day, a bomb at Herbert Park in Ballsbridge did very significant damage to a fountain in honour of King Edward VII, who had launched the International Exhibition there in 1907. In relation to the equestrian statues, *The Irish Times* believed that 'the efforts appear to have been made simultaneously, and without any great success.'[141] Still, King William III was removed from College Green, only to suffer another humiliating attack while in storage at the Corporation Yard on Hanover Street. As would happen to Lord Nelson a few decades later, raiders succeeded in stealing the head of the statue. It was reported on 11 December that: 'on Sunday night last a number of men entered the yard, sawed the head off, and took it away.'[142]

The monument to George II that withstood the 1928 bombing did eventually fall victim to a further bombing nine years later, in an attack that inflicted significantly more damage. It was reported then that 'the bronze equestrian statue of King George the Second, which had stood in the centre of the Green since 1758, was blown to pieces, and fragments of the granite pedestal were hurled thirty yards away.'[143]

Attacks in Dublin were not confined to statues, as other symbols and iconography attached to the days of British rule were also targeted. An example of this is the Royal Coat of Arms, or 'the lion and the unicorn', once common in the city. At half past six on a quiet November morning in 1937, an explosion destroyed the plaster cast of the Royal Coat of Arms at Exchange Court, with *The Irish Times* reporting that:

The force of the explosion broke the plaster cast of the lion and the unicorn into pieces, blew a large hole in the wall of the building, and shattered hundreds of panes of glass in surrounding houses, shops and offices. Bricks and mortar were hurled into rooms of the premises, smashing furniture and damaging official documents.[144]

Several monuments were removed by the State, and in some cases they were controversially given away or sold at low cost. The statue of King George I, which had originally stood on Essex Bridge before finding shelter in the Mansion House, ultimately ended up in Birmingham in 1937. The decision to allow the statue to leave Dublin was controversial at the time because, regardless of the political debate around it, it was seen as a fine example of the work of a celebrated sculptor.

The unveiling of the Queen Victoria statue. In 1948, work ultimately began on removing her from Leinster House.

The Leinster House monument of Queen Victoria was another that was removed from the city by those in authority and not republican bombers. This statue had proven particularly controversial as it was placed within the grounds of the national parliament. In February 1933, for example, members of Fianna Fáil made it to the pages of the national media when they outlined their belief that they considered having such a statue outside the Dáil to be 'inconsistent with the main objects of Fianna Fáil.' To them, it was baffling that 'this relic of imperialism should still disgrace the precincts of our Parliamentary institution.'[145]

In July 1948, work finally began on removing Victoria from Leinster Lawn. This marked the beginning of a process that would see Victoria end up in storage at the Royal Hospital Kilmainham for several years. Newspaper reports quoted the Taoiseach as saying that its removal was intended to provide parking space for cars. The process of removing Victoria took eight weeks. When being taken from Leinster House, Victoria had to be removed on her back, being too tall to pass through the gates otherwise. When in storage, there was an approach made by London, Ontario to acquire the statue for re-erection in Canada. *The Irish Times* outlined that the cost of transport was so high that Canadian interest waned.[146]

Today, this statue stands in Sydney, Australia, having essentially been gifted to the Australian people. Unusually, however, parts of it remain in Dublin, at Leinster House, Dublin Castle and Bully's Acre Cemetery.

In his history of the Irish Republican Army, Tim Pat Coogan discusses an IRA plot to bomb the Nelson Pillar in the late 1930s, which coincided with the decision of Sean Russell for the IRA to take over the authority of the 'Government of the Republic'. Russell remains a controversial figure in Irish republican history. From Fairvew, he participated in the Easter Rising, War of Independence and the subsequent Civil War. He would later attempt to procure arms for the IRA from Soviet Russia in the 1930s, though when this failed he sought military assistance from the Third Reich. He ultimately died on a German U-Boat that was destined for Ireland in 1940. Coogan claimed that:

> Peadar O'Flaherty, believed to be Russell's right-hand man, planned the explosion for a Saturday evening, when the street would normally be full of people. To avoid fatalities, he planned to set the explosives, withdraw and notify the police, giving time to cordon off the area.[147]

One IRA member of the time told Coogan that they quite literally walked down O'Connell Street with wads of gelignite on their persons, but on reaching the pillar it was discovered that the monument closed early to the public on Saturday evenings.[148] While this story comes directly from IRA volunteers of the time, it is remarkable that no subsequent attempt was made if the intelligence and explosives had been gathered for the task.

The 1940s and 1950s saw a wave of bombings against targets such as the Earl of Carlisle and Lord Gough in the Phoenix Park. The Gough statue in the park had been the victim of frequent assaults, and was even beheaded on Christmas Eve in 1945, but it was a blast in 1957 that would ultimately topple the Viscount. Following this assault, an anonymous poem began to circulate in the city, which some would claim was written by Brendan Behan. The poem was actually the work of Vincent Caprani, a Dublin printer and trade unionist from an Italian background. Caprani joked that:

> *There are strange things done from twelve to one*
> *In the hollow at Phaynix Park,*
> *There's maidens mobbed and gentlemen robbed*
> *In the bushes after dark;*

But the strangest of all within human recall
Concerns the statue of Gough,
It was a terrible fact, and a most wicked act,
For his bollix they tried to blow off![149]

An antique postcard of the Gough statue, bombed in 1957.

A popular song at the time entitled 'Gough's Immortal Statue', much like Caprani's poem, poked fun at the unfortunate monument, and even included a verse aimed at the O'Connell Street monument to Horatio Nelson:

When Nelson heard about it, he shouted to Parnell.
'How long will I be left here, now Charlie can you tell.
For I don't feel safe upon my seat,
for I may retreat down to the street,
like Gough's immortal statue, up near the Magazine.'[150]

The following year, the Earl of Carlisle was bombed, not far from the location where Gough's monument had stood. The republican movement distanced itself from this incident, noting that they were not concerned with monuments from the past but rather with contemporary political issues. Today, a visitor to the Phoenix Park can still see the location where the Earl of Carlisle's monument once stood. A statement from the Irish Republican Publicity Bureau distanced the movement from the attack, and a month later, when a bomb destroyed a monument to the Earl of Eglinton in St Stephen's Green, the Bureau issued a press release claiming that 'the creation of such incidents is against Republican policy, which is directed against British occupation of our country.'[151]

One of the most unusual chapters in the history of the pillar was a brazen attempt on it in October 1955 by students. The students came from University College Dublin, which was then located at Earlsfort Terrace. It was reported that:

> A group of university students forced their way to the top of the Nelson Pillar in O'Connell Street on Saturday afternoon, locked themselves in with a key which they had taken from the keeper, and hung out a huge banner of Kevin Barry. Thousands of afternoon shoppers watched the group cut a section of the safety cage at the top of the pillar and unfurl their banner. It took three hours to get them down.[152]

Nine students participated in the protest, which was later claimed by the National Students' Council. Interestingly, the students had actually plotted to destroy the statue, and it was reported that the men had 'flame guns' in their possession at the time of the attack.[153] Despite the intention to damage the pillar, and the presence of such weapons, nobody was arrested for their role in the incident.

Gardaí compiled a detailed report on the incident entitled 'Unlawful Assembly and Malicious Damage – Nelson Pillar – October 29 1955', which provides brilliant insight into those behind the attack.

Gardaí believed that the blame rested with two active IRA members:

> Joseph Christle may be regarded as the ring-leader in this matter. He is an active member of the I.R.A, as is Brendan Doyle, and it is likely that all the other students concerned are either members of the I.R.A or certainly active sympathisers. Christle has been very emphatic that the I.R.A organisation has no responsibility for this attempt and that he may be censured by I.R.A. Headquarters for taking part in it.[154]

William Bailham, the man tasked with the day-to-day running of the pillar as a tourist attraction, was paid sixpence each by five young men at about 2.30 p.m. on Saturday 29 October. Bailham was confronted by the men later when he went to inform them that their time was up, commenting on the state of the weather. When his keys were taken from him, Gardaí reported:

> Having got the keys, the gate was opened and Bailham saw some big oil cans being brought into the entrance hall and something long on sticks which resembled a rolled up blind. In a few minutes Bailham was informed by the young men that they were students and again assured him that everything, including the money, would be alright. To this Bailham replied 'how is it going to be alright when you're going to blow it up?'[155]

The young men informed Bailham they had absolutely no intention of blowing the pillar itself up, and he was told to go to Store Street and notify Gardaí that the pillar had been taken over.

At one point, a great cheer went up from the crowd that had gathered around the base when it was noticed that those on top had unfolded a large canvas, on which was depicted the head of a man, and underneath in large letters was the name 'Kevin Barry'.

Gardaí took nine names and addresses from the men involved. All were aged between 18 and 23, with the exception of Christle. Christle was later interviewed by Gardaí, and openly admitted to his role in the attack, even noting that he had already tested the flame guns on stone. In a list of items found on top of the Nelson Pillar, gardaí included five cans of oil resembling paraffin or diesel oil, one Morton Longley 'Tiger' flame gun, one 'Hauck' Flame Gun, one hurley, one brown paper bag containing seven packages of sandwiches and, of course, 'one canvas with painting of Kevin Barry thereon.' The young students were not prosecuted, gardaí noting that 'It is evident they are looking for publicity, and it is thought they will welcome being prosecuted, in which case they do not anticipate being sentenced.'[156]

William P. Fogarty was spokesperson for the National Students' Council, and in the aftermath of the event he told the media that 'the sooner we go ahead with the job of removing every symbol of British rule in Ireland, the sooner we can make Ireland, in fact, what she is of right – queen of her own affairs.'[157]

In the aftermath of the student protest, the Gaelic League backed their call for the removal of Horatio with a motion passed at their annual general meeting. The proposer of the motion stated that 'it was shameful to retain the memorial to Nelson in Dublin's principal street, while the memory of so many of our patriot dead remained un-commemorated.'[158]

8. The Eighth of March, 1966

'The official view would appear to be that the explosion is not part of any new political campaign, that it was carried out by a "fringe" organisation of Republican militants, by a small group rather than a national group.'
  – The Irish Times' report on the bombing.[159]

*I*n a *Newsbeat* special for RTÉ Television that was rebroadcast in the aftermath the 1966 bombing of the Nelson Pillar, Frank Hall stated that Nelson was, in many ways, 'a stranger, stranded on a foreign shore, left behind by the receding tide of Empire.' In a sign of changing times and the modern world, the caretaker of the pillar joked with Hall that 'some people come in and look for an elevator' when they heard of just how many steps were within the monument. Below Nelson, Ireland was changing and modernising in many ways, and to most he had become a normal enough part of the skyline. As the caretaker of the pillar would tell RTÉ, though, it was 'Spaniards, Frenchmen, Germans, Dutchmen, South Americans, all kinds of American people, Australians and New Zealanders' who visited in droves, as much as locals. 'If one of ours was up there, do you think people would still go up?' Hall asked the caretaker, who replied that it was

The aftermath of the republican bomb, captured by Pól Ó Duibhir.

first and foremost the view and not the man that brought people to the pillar.[160]

To some, however, Nelson remained not just a viewing platform over the city, but rather an imperialist symbol, and his ultimate demise would coincide with the fiftieth anniversary of the Easter Rising, one of the most celebrated and important moments in the republican historic calendar. Indeed, the event became the most dramatic and discussed moment of the anniversary, greatly overshadowing the State commemoration of the rebellion. As Roisin Higgins, a historian who has studied the anniversary in great detail, has noted, the bombing of the pillar became 'a means through which all authority could be mocked. The credibility of the state was shaken by the act of violence at the heart of the capital city.'[161] This chapter will examine the bombing of the pillar on 8 March 1966, looking at some of the myths that have emerged around the act, and also looking at the response of the State, the media and the republican movement to the incident.

On the morning of 8 March 1966, at 1.30 a.m., O'Connell Street was rocked by a powerful explosion. The power of the blast brought the top half of the Nelson Pillar crashing into the street, with the Admiral himself shattering on impact with the ground. A statement was quickly issued by the Government Information Bureau for publication, in which it was stated that:

> The Minister for Justice, Mr. Brian Lenihan T.D., condemned the reckless action of those responsible for the blowing up of Nelson's Pillar. The Minister pointed out that the explosion was timed for 1.30 a.m., when it was well known that many persons, including late-night workers in restaurants and dance halls, would be in the O'Connell Street area.[162]

In the panic that followed the O'Connell Street explosion, armed detectives were placed on duty around monuments that were deemed likely targets of attack, including the Wellington monument in the Phoenix Park and the War

Memorial Gardens at Islandbridge. It was reported in the media that shop owners in the area of the pillar were actually expecting a boost in business, as 'country people visiting the city would be drawn to the area to see the damaged Pillar.'[163]

On the day following the bombing, media reports placed great emphasis on the 'expert' nature of the job. The pillar and Nelson's statue had blown upwards and not outwards, which explained the minimal damage to the streetscape. A ballistics expert told *The Irish Times* that the job was a very clean one, pointing towards the use of plastic explosives, and told the paper that 'the whole charge could have been prepared away from the site, then brought there and stuck in position in a few moments.'[164] The *Irish Independent* reported that Lieut. Colonel Patrick McCourt, Senior Explosives Officer of the Irish Army, climbed the remnants of the pillar an hour after the explosion, and described the bombing as a 'formidable task'. The front page of the paper also described Stephen Maugham, a taxi man, as the luckiest man in the city. Maugham had been sitting in his taxi at the traffic lights next to the pillar, and described witnessing 'a cloud of rocks falling towards him.'[165]

The reaction of the British media to the bombing was mixed, though *The Economist* made its feelings perfectly clear, writing that:

> Anti-colonialism could go no further than to defy an occupying army that ceased occupation 50 years ago by putting plastic explosives under a naval hero 150 years dead. Nelson's fall may be good for a laugh; but it is comical only by the greatest good luck. Post-colonial Dubliners being safely in their beds by 1.30 a.m., nobody was hurt.[166]

What remained of Johnston's Doric column, captured
by Pól Ó Duibhir.

The *Irish Press*
reports the
news, captured
by Pól Ó
Duibhir.

The brother of the then-present Lord Nelson was quoted in the *Irish Press* as expressing great regret at the time, believing that 'so many people associated it with the centre of Dublin.' Another member of the Nelson family described it as 'a horrible thing – something that we could have done without in a world already full of horror.'[167]

While *The Economist* and the Nelsons took the explosion very seriously, contemporary newspaper reports indicate a very different feeling on O'Connell Street. Readers of one American newspaper, for example, were informed that:

> Dublin's mood was one of gaiety. Crowds jostled and joked around the police cordons at the scene. Said a newsvendor who was near the column as it was blasted:

> 'Within minutes hundreds of people had flocked to the scene. Nobody seemed shocked. The crowd was laughing and there were shouts of 'Nelson has lost his last battle!'[168]

Life goes on as the clean-up begins, captured by Pól Ó Duibhir.

Unsurprisingly, inside the Oireachtas there was widespread condemnation of the bombing, though the most severe condemnation of the bombers would not come until 1969, when Senator Owen Dudley Edwards spoke at length about the meaning of the monument to him, and the decline of Dublin in recent times:

> When in 1966 the pillar was half blown down by a person or persons unknown, I, as a Dubliner, felt a sense of loss, not because of Nelson – one could hardly see Nelson at the top – but because this pillar symbolised for many Dubliners the centre of the city. It had a certain rugged, elegant grace about it, apart from the kind of little cage at the top which was there to prevent people jumping off. It had a rugged, elegant grace about it which marked the city as something different from a city which had grown mushroom-like in the last few decades.
>
> The pillar went back to the early days of the 19th Century and most people would agree, when looking

at prints of old Dublin showing O'Connell Street, Upper O'Connell Street or Sackville Street, the old O'Connell Bridge, which was first called Carlisle Bridge, with the pillar in the background, they see the city and O'Connell Street with a grace which is sadly lacking today. The only thing of elegance left in O'Connell Street now apart from the statue of O'Connell, and one can argue about that, although I personally have rather an affection for it, is the General Post Office. O'Connell Street now has a ring of Piccadilly Circus about it, with the new buildings, which have been erected to replace the destroyed ones, covered in advertising matter. The man who destroyed the pillar made Dublin look more like

This Walker Collection shot shows what remained of the Nelson Pillar following the bombing. Courtesy of the National Library of Ireland.

Birmingham and less like an ancient city on the River Liffey, because the presence of the pillar gave Dublin an internationally known appearance.[169]

The explosion caused by republicans on 8 March left the remainder of the Nelson Pillar standing there in the street as a bizarre sightseeing attraction. This created problems for authorities, who understood, quite rightly, that any controlled demolition was likely to inflict more damage on the street than the initial explosion had, with the charge closer to the ground. Tony Killian, a technical engineer with the explosive supply industry who was there during the controlled demolition on 15 March, detailed the preparations that went into it in a 2009 article:

> With Garda permission I arrived on site at 9pm on Sunday March 14th and was introduced to Comdt. Seward of the Army Corps of Engineers. He told me that he was ordered to travel to Dublin, shown the remains of the Pillar and was issued with a simple instruction: 'demolish that'.

On the day of the explosion, Killian had permission to shelter in a doorway in North Earl Street, only seventy yards or so from the remains of the monument. He noted that the noise level surpassed his expectations and delighted the general public, who 'had been promised a "dull thud" and in typical Dublin fashion they raised a resounding cheer.' Killian tackled the myth that the army had broken every window on the street; a great Dublin story that doesn't hold up to scrutiny. At £4,180 19*s.* 10*d.*, the damage claims from the second explosion were less than a quarter of those from the initial blast.[170]

In the folklore of Dublin, the IRA is said to have blown up the pillar. In reality, however, the IRA distanced itself totally from the bombing. A statement from the 'Republican Movement' in the aftermath of the event said:

> The Republican Movement has not concerned itself in the slightest way with the destruction of monuments of foreign origin, nor has the movement aided implicitly or explicitly such demolitions. We have refused to settle for the destruction of the symbols of domination; we are interested in the destruction of the domination itself.[171]

At the time, various rumours in relation to the explosion spread across the city of Dublin. Some placed the blame on foreign revolutionaries. Archaeologist Franc Myles, who would later excavate the site of the Nelson Pillar, recalled in an article on the site that:

> The explosion that demolished most of the pillar was for several years afterwards rumoured to be the work of Basque nationalists engaged in a hands-on training exercise with some local republicans of a socialist bent. It is recognised now, however, that by the mid-'60s the Basques were probably more au fait with the use of explosives than their Irish counterparts.[172]

The bombing of the Nelson Pillar is now known to have been the action of one-time members of what was known as the 'Christle Group': a network of republican activists built around the charismatic Joe Christle. Christle was a Dublin republican activist who had partaken in IRA cross-border raids in the 1950s on Armagh and Omagh, and who served as editor of the *United Irishman* newspaper for a brief period. Christle was a qualified barrister and accountant, who would become a college lecturer and a sports administrator during a long and colourful life. Christle had been instrumental in the establishment of the National Students' Council; the very same organisation that had attacked the pillar in 1955. As an IRA volunteer, Christle had been shot during a raid on Omagh, and his courage was never doubted by those above him, even if his wisdom was. Robert William White, biographer of republican Ruairí Ó Brádaigh, has described Christle as a 'maverick' who opposed an IRA leadership that he believed to be 'too conservative'.[173] Ignorant of the upcoming IRA Border Campaign, Christle was pushing for more and more action against British forces in Northern Ireland. As many have noted, splits in the history of the republican movement are endemic, and a split was the natural outcome of the tension between Christle and the leadership. As Lawrence William White has noted in the *Dictionary of Irish Biography*:

> Suspicious of Christle's long-term ambitions, and fearful that his recklessness might imperil preparations for the planned border campaign (of which he and his clique were completely ignorant), GHQ ordered his expulsion from the IRA (June 1956), on the technicality of his having addressed a Sinn Féin meeting without authorisation. Launching a rival Oglaigh na hÉireann, which siphoned off half the IRA's Dublin unit, including most of the officers and the most capable volunteers, Christle formed a loose alliance with Saor Uladh, the armed republican faction led by Liam Kelly in east Co. Tyrone, their combined forces comprising some seventy men.[174]

This alliance of disenfranchised republicans was capable of carrying out attacks on a small scale against British interests, for example attacking six unmanned customs huts along the border in November 1956. This action had been carried out on Remembrance Sunday, a day that had a long history of republican action and agitation in Ireland. The IRA leadership took the threat of Christle's group seriously, believing that any attempt by the State to suppress that faction would have implications for their own organisation. A great deal of effort and resources was spent on attempting to monitor the splinter groups and build intelligence around them. For the IRA figure tasked with shadowing Christle, however, the task was far from simple, as the champion cyclist 'regularly sped away from him on his modern racing bike.'[175]

One republican who followed Christle was Liam Sutcliffe, who had joined the IRA in 1954, and is the only member of the group to have publicly spoken of the attack on the Nelson Pillar. Liam first spoke publicly of his role in the attack in 2000, in an interview that was aired by RTÉ, which led to his questioning by Gardaí and a media frenzy. In 2003, Liam watched the Spire of Light being put in place on O'Connell Street, and praised it as 'a much better thing to have on the main street than an old foreign admiral with a broken arm and a missing leg.'[176] Liam claimed in an interview at the time that the idea to destroy the pillar had emerged during a discussion in a bar on the Crumlin Road in Belfast, out of a belief that the jubilee of the Easter Rising would be better marked by removing the Admiral than 'functions and dinners' organised by the State. The first attempt to bomb the pillar was not the March explosion, however, but an earlier attempt on the last day of February, which had failed to detonate. The dangerous process of removing the 'mine', as Sutcliffe described it, involved returning to the pillar on 1 March.

On examining the device, Sutcliffe found that it was, in his own words, 'wrongly wired, plus they used a bicycle battery'[177], and he spent a week 'redesigning' the device before returning it to the pillar.

'Cleaner Streets Please', captured by Pól Ó Duibhir.

The operation was code-named 'Operation Humpty Dumpty', and Sutcliffe insists that a combination of gelignite and ammonal was used to destroy the pillar. Not a man to watch his own work unfold, he returned home, and was asleep at the time of the explosion on 8 March, reading of its success later in the pages of the national media. Sutcliffe remained active in republican politics, joining Saor Éire in 1970. Blessed with a keen sense of humour, he described the desire of Gardaí to speak with him in 2000 about the bombing as being akin to 'someone being arrested in the 1950s for taking over the GPO in 1916.'[178]

While the involvement of Sutcliffe in the incident is undeniable, a very colourful claim of involvement came from the pages of *Ringolevio,* the story of Emmett Grogan. Grogan was a central figure in the Diggers, a radical community in San Francisco who organised community events like free food distribution, and even organised free concerts where acts like the Grateful Dead and Janis Joplin performed. Bob Dylan's 1978 album *Street Legal* was dedicated to the memory of Grogan, considered an eccentric but leading figure in the arts and counter-cultural scenes of 1960s America. This American radical spent some time in Dublin in the 1960s, which he documented in his book, claiming to have been recruited in a Dublin boozer to the task of lookout on O'Connell Street on the night of Horatio Nelson's departure. Grogan claimed that men were positioned in key locations and 'they turned away men and women and cars and cabs and told them to go somewhere else', and noted that the head of Nelson was 'taken away and transported to the backyard of a well-known saloonkeeper where it remained on private display' for some time afterwards.[179] This account is wonderfully written, but doesn't quite hold up, as of course, Nelson's head was taken to a Dublin Corporation lock-up. Much to the dismay of the city authorities, it would vanish soon afterwards.

9. Souvenir-Hunters and Chart-Toppers

'The most notorious and improbable "antique" of the year went on exhibition yesterday in a dingy antique bazaar in Barrett Street, in the West End of London.'

— *The Times* welcomes
Nelson's head to London.[180]

From the moment the explosion detonated on O'Connell Street, in the true spirit of the city, the frantic scramble for

In the process of destruction, image by Pól Ó Duibhir.

souvenirs and relics of the iconic monument began. Just as Dubliners had looted the department shops around the pillar fifty years earlier in the midst of rebellion, the entrepreneurial spirit of the city came to the fore again. This image captures the spirit of the free-for-all on O'Connell Street, and was captured by Pól Ó Duibhir. Describing it for me, he noted that 'The man seems to be performing as a social service and the other guy is toasting the occasion with a cuppa. One lady behind already has a piece of the Pillar in her hand.'

Taking what they can. This image was snapped by Pól Ó Duibhir.

While many Dubliners were content with small pieces of the pillar, others had their eye on larger sections. The comedy actor John Molloy, for example, succeeded in liberating Nelson of his sword, taking it from the rubble on the night of the explosion. A week later, he appeared in the *Sunday Independent* clutching it in a Nelson-like pose, with a closed eye and a hidden hand. 'He brought what was left of the sword before the TV cameras on the Late Late Show and told the story of how he found it', and Molloy told the media that he would use the sword as a prop in his upcoming one-man show at the Gate, *Old Segocia*.[181] Today, Nelson's sword remains at large.

One part of Nelson that remains on display before the people of Dublin is the head of the statue that stood on top of the pillar, but it too has been on something of a journey. In the aftermath of the explosion, the head was taken to a Corporation yard in Ardee Street, though it was stolen soon afterwards by students from the National College of Art and Design, with workmen discovering that the head had gone missing on the morning of 18 March. The young raiders forced their way into the premises, before very politely leaving the sum of £2 for damages caused, as well as a list of damages, with a Dublin newspaper. The *Irish Press* reported that the theft was being investigated by Kevin Street Gardaí[182], but the taking of the head only began a cat-and-mouse pursuit, which would even see Nelson's head taken to London.

Thirteen years after the theft of Nelson's head, one of the students involved told the story to a journalist from *The Irish Times*. 'It boiled down to the fact that the Student Union in the college was very short of money, and we realised that if we could lay our hands on it we could make a lot of money out of it in the publicity', the man remarked. The head was constantly on the move, even making an appearance on stage with The Dubliners, and Pól Ó Duibhir witnessed the students at Killiney Beach:

> One day in late March, 1966, I was walking along the station road in Killiney when my eye was

caught by something unusual happening near the waterline in front of Homan's.

One of Homan's long rowing boats was partly drawn up on the beach and seemed to be flanked by balaclava-wearing figures presenting oars. It was too far away to be sure of what was going on.

I had my camera across my shoulder and I set out for Homan's. When I got there the action, whatever it had been, was clearly over and there were just a few ordinary-looking people hanging around. I was convinced, however, that something had been going on, so I started photographing what remained.

The boat was still there but there were no balaclavas and no oars. There was an odd-looking sack which clearly contained something very heavy. I thought of a body but figured it wouldn't fit. It was heavy enough, though, to leave a deep trail in the sand.[183]

The rather unusual spectacle only made sense when, soon afterwards, on 2 April, the *Evening Press* carried an image of Nelson's head on Killiney beach, appearing as a fashion shot, with two stylish young ladies patched into the image. A trip to Killiney was one thing, but Nelson was destined for London, with the young students bringing the head (via Northern Ireland) to Benny Gray, a London antique shop owner who offered a generous rent payment to display the head in his shop.

There was plenty of confusion surrounding just who had Nelson's head, with Butty Sugrue claiming that he had the real head securely held in Dublin, with the ultimate

**Students with Nelson's head at Killiney. This image was
snapped by Pól Ó Duibhir.**

aspiration of displaying it in his London pub, the aptly
named Admiral Nelson pub in Kilburn. 'Nobody would
dare steal my head', Sugrue was quoted as saying in the
newspapers at the time, and perhaps he was right – this
was after all the famous Butty Sugrue who had pulled
buses along with his teeth, and could lift a man using
only one hand.[184] Gray had no fear of Sugrue, however,
telling a British newspaper that 'If he were to question the
authenticity of a glass of stout I was drinking, then I would
take notice of what he was saying. He is a publican – I am
in the antiques business.'[185]

While Sugrue may have desperately sought the
attention of owning Nelson's head, Gray had done a
deal with the students, and the head went on display
in his premises, even being examined by an art expert

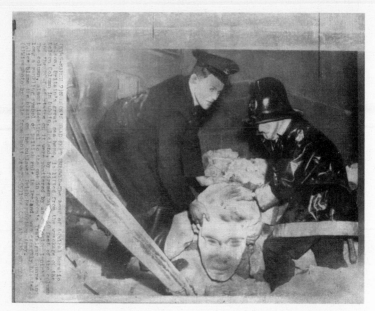

Dublin Fire Brigade men remove the head of Nelson from the rubble. Notice that it has been 'touched up' for publication.

from the famous Christie's auction house, who stated that it was certainly over 100 years old. Gray basked in the media attention that came with the temporary ownership of the head, and it was reported on 2 May that Lord Nelson was wearing lipstick.[186] At home, as time wore on, questions began to be asked about when the head would be returned. According to the student interviewed years later, when Gardaí began arresting students who had no involvement in the affair, it became clear that it was time to return the head to Dublin. On 6 September, Mr Gray arrived in Dublin in spectacular fashion, with a slow-moving lorry pulling up alongside the General Post Office on O'Connell Street. Gray was joined by The Dubliners, who performed a reworked version of their song 'Nelson's Farewell', reported in the media as 'Nelson's Return'. Mr Gray asked into a hand-held megaphone whether any custodians of the pillar were present, and the head was returned to a confused Corporation official. It was a suitably bizarre end to the saga of the art students. In the years that followed, they led a variety of interesting lives. A star in the popular TV show 'The Riordans' and a future lecturer in the NCAD were among the entrepreneurs who saw a golden opportunity that they couldn't resist. The Corporation insisted that Nelson's head was to do no more travelling, but he has been on the move ever since. City Hall, the Civic Museum on South William Street and the Dublin City Library and Archive on Pearse Street have all hosted the head of Horatio. Today, Pearse Street seems his ultimate destination, making him a southsider far from home.

NCAD students pose with the stolen head.

Today, chunks of the pillar have ended up in the homes and gardens of Dubliners across the city, with the author aware of pieces in Cabra, Inchicore and elsewhere. One of the most innovative uses of the remains of the pillar discovered whilst researching this book was in Killester, where a Dublin Corporation worker constructed his garden steps from the remains of Francis Johnston's monument. His daughter informed me:

My dad, Bill Armstrong, worked for Dublin Corporation when the Pillar was blown up in 1966. He worked on the clear up and took a number of quite large pieces of the granite column back to our house in Killester in his van, along with other pieces of the rubble. He then built the garden step which is still there to this day, using four of the granite blocks and some of the rubble.

Bill Armstrong's steps in Killester today. With thanks to Brenda Armstrong Kelleher.

There was a field day for would-be Bill Armstrongs when the remains of the pillar were dumped in St Anne's Estate in Raheny, with newspapers reporting eager crowds gathering to collect pieces. Corporation officials dumped the rubble in a number of locations. Paddy Nugent, a Corporation official, posed with the remains of the figure in Nelson mode for the cameras, perhaps inspired by the recent image of actor John Molloy published in the *Sunday Independent*.

Some of the most exciting remains of the pillar to be seen today are outside the capital, at Butler House in Kilkenny. There, slabs of the beautiful stone have taken on a new life as a place to sit and rest, with letters that once spelled out the naval victories of Nelson still visible. There are other pieces to be found across the island, including in museums – for example, The Little

Paddy Nugent strikes a pose. With thanks to Margaret Nugent.

Museum of Dublin possesses a small piece of the pillar, which was loaned to the Tate Gallery in London in 2013 for an exhibition on iconoclasm.

Pieces of the pillar at Butler House today. Thanks to James Nolan.

To those hoarding the pillar, the author still seeks a chunk for his own back garden!

Songs Inspired by the Bombing.

Physical pieces of the pillar are one way in which Dubliners are reminded of the monument in their day-to-day lives, but seven-inch music singles are definitely another. In the aftermath of the Nelson Pillar explosion, a number of singles were written, largely mocking the demise of the pillar. *Sing*, 'Britain's folk song magazine', commented in June 1966: 'what a load of folklore has come out of that O'Connell Street explosion'[187], and reprinted the words of Tommy Makem's 'The Death of Nelson'. To the tune of 'The Sash My Father Wore', an anthem of Irish loyalism, Makem's song was good-humoured, but perpetuated the idea that the IRA had caused the explosion, noting that 'He thought the Irish liked him, or they wouldn't let him stay – That is except those blighters they call the IRA!'

Of the singles produced in the aftermath of the bombing, none had the same impact as 'Up Went Nelson', composed by four Belfast schoolteachers. Gerry Burns, Finbar Carolan, John Sullivan and Eamonn McGirr enjoyed weeks at the top of the Irish charts, ahead of acts like Dusty Springfield and Cher. The song joked of the longstanding controversies around the pillar, noting:

> *The Irish population came from miles around*
> *To see the English hero lying on the ground*
> *The Dublin Corporation had no funds to have it done*
> *But the Pillar blew to pieces by the ton, ton, ton!*

The Dubliners made great capital off the event, with the head appearing onstage with them at the Gate Theatre

nelson's farewell

the foggy dew

TRA P9

THE DUBLINERS

'Nelson's Farewell', a successful single for The Dubliners.

not long after it had vanished from the Corporation yard. Interestingly, in his autobiography, Ronnie Drew recounted how he personally had gone to the top of the pillar with a friend only a few short years before the explosion, but there was no sentimental longing for its return in their hit single. The song was written by 'Galway Joe' Dolan, a name used by the writer to differentiate himself from the popular Mullingar singer of the same name. Dolan was of very solid traditional music stock, having been a founding member of the band Sweeney's Men. In 'Nelson's Farewell', Dolan placed the event in the context of world news, and the space race that was underway between the superpowers of capitalism and communism:

> *Oh the Russians and the Yanks, with lunar probes they play,*
> *Toora loora loora loora loo!*
> *And I hear the French are trying hard to make up lost headway,*
> *Toora loora loora loora loo!*
> *But now the Irish join the race,*
> *We have an astronaut in space,*
> *Ireland, boys, is now a world power too!*
> *So let's sing our celebration,*
> *It's a service to the nation.*
> *So poor old Admiral Nelson, toora loo!*

Certainly, on the airwaves and in the public mind, the explosion and the media frenzy that followed it was a central part of the 1966 anniversary of the Easter rebellion. As Roisin Higgins has noted, 'the unofficial strike became a means through which all authority could be mocked'[188], and the light-hearted hit singles and student escapades that followed the bombing only added to that feeling.

10. *Replacing Nelson*

Ian Ritchie's 2003 Spire of Light is visible behind Oisin Kelly's celebrated 1970s sculpture of trade unionist Jim Larkin, May Day 2013. Image by Paul Reynolds.

*I*n the decades that followed the destruction of the Nelson Pillar, there was much discussion among Dublin Corporation, the government and indeed the general public over what, if anything, should stand where the Nelson monument did for generations.

The Nelson Pillar Act (1969) transferred control of the site to the Corporation, but at a significant cost in compensation to the Trustees of the Nelson Pillar. The Act was largely controversy-free, although Owen Sheehy-Skeffington did use the discussion around it to attack the authorities for not opting to preserve what remained of the pillar, stating:

> I believe if a monument which one wants to preserve, or a house which one wants to preserve, is damaged and is capable of repair, there is no excuse for saying: 'This house is in a dangerous condition, let us blow up the rest of it.' I believe a pillar or a house, if damaged, can be shored up and preserved even if it is in a shaken condition. In fact, the base of the Pillar was so solid and the Pillar was so narrow in comparison with it that I do not believe there was any real danger which could not have been met by a shoring up which would not take more than a few hours. I believe the Pillar could have been re-assembled and rebuilt.[189]

An emerging trend in the years that followed the bombing was for campaign groups to call for the erection of a monument to another individual on the site, just as campaigners had attempted to replace the Nelson statue during the lifetime of the structure. Arthur Griffith was proposed in 1970 as a suitable replacement for the pillar, with the Arthur Griffith Society putting this forward.

Griffith, founder of the Sinn Féin party in 1907, was something of a controversial choice, owing to his role in Civil War-era politics and the signing of the Anglo-Irish Treaty. Griffith was memorialised, along with Michael Collins, with the erection of a memorial at the back of Leinster House in 1923.[190]

Patrick Pearse was also proposed in the 1970s, with the centenary of his birth in 1879 approaching. Dublin Corporation debated the placement of a forty-foot-high monument to Pearse at the site, with the architect Gary Trimble submitting a design that showed Pearse reading to three children, celebrating his role as an educator. While Trimble's design was not chosen, the Corporation debated another model for a Pearse monument at the site in that same year. Architect Yann Goulet brought forward a proposed monument that would contain over £150,000 worth of bronze, and stand taller than the neighbouring General Post Office. The attitude of elected Dublin Corporation members was clear quite quickly, with Councillor Frank Sherwin stating that 'it should be thrown in the Liffey', while Councillor Hanna Barlow described it as 'the yoke'. Once again, planning permission was refused by the Corporation, ensuring that the debate on the site would continue. Goulet may have simply been described as an architect in the media at the time, though in reality he was a Breton nationalist who had collaborated with fascism during the Second World War. At the time of his passing in 1999, the *Guardian* noted in his obituary that: 'After the liberation of France, Goulet, with his wife and two children, made his way to Ireland, via Wales. Thus he was absent when a court in Rennes sentenced him to death for collaboration.'[191] Goulet enjoyed a successful career in Ireland, and the monument to the Dublin Brigade of the IRA at the rear of the Custom House is one example of his work with which Dubliners may be familiar.

1987 saw the Dublin Metropolitan Streets Commission propose that the pillar be rebuilt, albeit without the statue of Horatio Nelson. To the chairman of the group, 'the Pillar was more than a monument, it was the symbol of the city, and Dublin hasn't been the same since it was blown up 21 years ago.'[192]

In 1988, to coincide with Dublin's 'Millennium' festival, the Smurfit Millennium Fountain was unveiled on O'Connell Street, which was known as the Anna Livia to Dubliners. Unveiled near to the Nelson Pillar site, it was condemned by leading sculptor Edward Delaney as an 'atrocious eyesore', who went as far as to say 'it's just a joke, like something out of Myles na gCopaleen.'[193]

'The Pillar Project', launched in 1988, aimed to spark a real discussion on just what should replace the pillar. As Yvonne Whelan has noted, however, this popular competition 'was only ever intended to be a generator of ideas and it was never planned to erect the winning design.'[194] The Pillar Project was open to all, and brought artists and architects together in collaboration. 'Both disciplines, and the public they are meant to serve, will benefit from the process', wrote Shane O'Toole, convenor of the project, at the time.[195] The proposals were all exhibited before the public in the General Post Office, and a public ballot was taken there, with the results to be declared on *The Late Late Show.*

Some of the entries and ideas to this high-profile competition drew strongly on the pillar and its legacy. The architects Sheila O'Donnell and John Tuomey, for example, proposed a piece of public art that would rise to an even greater height than the pillar, but which would contain a public telescope at Nelson's eye-level, allowing a visitor to enjoy the view of Lord Nelson, 'so that the vista of the city and Dublin Bay with the backdrops of the mountains can be enjoyed.'[196] The engineer Seán Mulcahy, with the help of the artist Eamonn O'Doherty, proposed a 110-metre-tall flagpole, flying a flag that would be 'perhaps the world's largest' in the centre of O'Connell Bridge. The flag could be raised and lowered by an operator daily, providing 'a twice-daily spectacle'.[197] One entry, which was ahead of its time, was the 'Millennium Arch', a dream of architect Michael Kinsella and artist Daniel McCarthy, to construct an arch not unlike the Arc de Triomphe, topped by a sculpture of an eternal flame, 'symbolic of a city where the spirit is never extinguished, despite the passing of time.'[198] The proposal was complementary to the neighbouring GPO, whereas other proposals would have dwarfed Francis Johnston's historic building once more. Not surprisingly, the public chose this as their ideal replacement for the pillar. Still, the result sadly stood for nothing, and Dublin was not to have her Arc de Triomphe.

O'Connell Street, by the late 1980s, was very much seen as a street in decline. The architect Thomas Murphy argued in 1993 that 'it has been identified in the public mind as being both dirty and dangerous.' Murphy put forward an ambitious proposal to build a 'Tower of Light' on the site, a fifty-metre-high structure with a viewing platform, returning a much-missed view to Dubliners. Described as a 'tubular truss steel structure, clad in glass', the proposed work enjoyed the support of the chief executive of the City Centre Business Association, who believed that it would give a new lease of life to a street badly in need of new energy.[199]

By the 1990s, the idea of building a monument akin to the pillar once more with a new figure on top of it was back on the agenda. The Progressive Democrats proposed that a monument be constructed on the site of the old pillar topped by a statue of James Joyce. To them, Joyce was 'the quintessential Dubliner, whose works celebrate Dublin as no other city has ever been celebrated in modern literature.' They also argued that being 'non-political, non-military, non-sectarian, and non-divisive', he was ideal for the site.[200] The Progressive Democrats' idea of placing a Dubliner on top of a new pillar would likely have enjoyed more support than that put forward in the pages of the *Western People*. There, it was reported that the Mayo Association wished to erect a 300-foot tower on the site of the former monument, to the memory of Mayo radical Michael Davitt. This monument would have stood twice as tall as the pillar had, and to fund it the Association planned to seek £2 million in costs from the European Union! Such a plan was nothing if not ambitious.[201]

Eventually, progress seemed to be on the cards. An international competition launched in 1998 received huge media attention, both at home and abroad. This competition, unlike the Pillar Project a decade earlier, would see its winning entry constructed on the site. The brief of those who entered the competition was clear: 'The monument shall have a vertical emphasis, an elegant structure of 21st century contemporary design which shall relate to the quality and scale of O'Connell Street as represented by the late 18th and early 20th century architecture.'

The competition received an impressive 205 entries, which was narrowed down to three architectural firms. Of these, two were British-based, while one was a Dublin firm.

Frank McDonald, longstanding campaigner for the regeneration of the city and journalist with *The Irish Times,* praised the winning design from London architect Ian Ritchie in glowing terms:

This sensational structure will redefine the city centre and people's perceptions of where that is, quite apart from providing Dublin with a new icon. It addresses not only its immediate context in O'Connell Street, but also more distant views and even the city as a whole. One of Mr Ritchie's 'fundamental objectives' was to lift people's spirits, and it will certainly do that.[202]

Here, the detail in Ian Ritchie's work is clearly visible.
Image by Paul Reynolds.

Sociologist Mary Corcoran has noted that, in relation to the work, 'The Spire represents a vehicle both for the economic revalorisation of the northern side of the river and the expression of a new kind of national and urban narrative.'[203] Just as the Nelson Pillar had expressed the ideology and aspirations of the Dublin elite who erected it, the new monument could be seen to represent the aspirations of Celtic Tiger Dublin. The monument, as Corcoran has noted, is undoubtedly part of a commodity culture.

Ian Ritchie was a long-established figure in international architecture. Among his works are the Reina Sofia Museum of Modern Art in Madrid, the Leipzig Messe Glass Hall, the Louvre Sculpture Courts and Pyramids, the Jubilee Line Extension and International Regatta Centre in London and the Royal Shakespeare Company Courtyard Theatre.

While Ritchie's winning proposal was widely praised, there was some opposition to the plan. Mícheál Ó Núalláin emerged as the leading voice of opposition to the project. Ó Núalláin, the brother of a certain Myles na gCopaleen, launched a court action to attempt to halt the planned project, as did the sculptor Mary Dunivya. These two separate actions were united in their belief that the winning design was not fitting for its urban environment. To Dunivya, what was proposed was an 'anorexic alien body; alien from every angle in material, size, shape and symbolism.'[204] Ó Núalláin's case received huge publicity and, blessed with the wit of his brother, Ó Núalláin believed that the monument would reduce O'Connell Street to 'an absurd Lilliputian dimension', and drew comparisons between the process that had led to the construction of the Nelson Pillar and the process that was used to select the Spire of Light. Journalist John Drennan quizzed Ó Núalláin on his opposition to Ritchie's work, and Ó Núalláin told him of his research on the former monument:

> I looked it up ... the monument was paid for by the ... British ascendancy ... It had little or nothing

to do with the Irish people ... the gas thing is the French were allies of Ireland. Now we have something similar, only the Irish people are paying for it ... a thing that is being made in England, imported to Ireland, and dumped on O'Connell St. It's undemocratic. Eighty public submissions have been made against the monument, three for.[205]

In a June 2000 letter to *The Irish Times,* Ó Núalláin went as far as to state that in the event of a autumn general election being called in Ireland, he was considering running as a 'stop the spike' candidate.[206] Ó Núalláin was not the only high-profile opponent of the Spire; his scepticism was shared by Daithí Hanley, a former city architect, and well-known writer Ulick O'Connor. Ó Núalláin even attempted to bring the issue to the attention of the European Commission, though ultimately his campaign was unsuccessful.

Prior to work on Ian Ritchie's Spire commencing, the site was excavated in 2001, with Franc Myles later writing of this experience and describing, not only the dig itself, but the interaction with Dubliners on a daily basis, many of whom felt a strong connection to the site and recalled the pillar. The 2001 excavation brought to the fore a renewed interest in the pillar among the general public, and a tale that a 'time capsule' had been placed within the foundations of the monument in the early nineteenth century captured the imagination of Dubliners. Myles recalled an elderly gentleman in a Crombie coat appearing daily at the site, peering down and asking whether 'the coins' had yet been found. In Myles' words:

The recovery of the foundation stone generated considerable public and media interest. Even as

> the stone was being prepared for its journey to
> the conservation lab, the press was pushing the
> time capsule story despite all initial evidence to
> the contrary. Exiting the hoarding that evening,
> we pushed through crowds of bystanders who
> appeared to be there by word of mouth alone.[207]

Just like the mythology that had grown around the bombing of the pillar in 1966, there was no truth to it, and thus no elusive coins to be found. Still, for a few weeks in 2001, the pillar was back on the minds and tongues of Dubliners.

Ian Ritchie's monument, which it was originally believed would be in place in 2000, was eventually completely in place by January 2003. It had gone up in six sections, and on 22 January 2003, thousands applauded as the final part of the work was put in place. There was a certain irony in the fact that the Lord Mayor of Dublin, who was in attendance on the day, had initially voted against the proposal when the Council were asked for their view on it in 1999. Having changed his tune, he now regarded it as 'something brave we wouldn't have done 20 years ago.'[208]

Conclusion

The humour of the natives would ensure that Ian Ritchie's monument would come to be known by any name but its own. Yet, regardless of what they jokingly call it, the locals have certainly come to accept it. In 2003, shiny and new, it stood as something of a declaration of Ireland's economic confidence and strength. Some see it today as a relic of the Celtic Tiger; a time when millions could be spent on a stainless steel pole. Others, however, see it as a beautiful work, evident by the commentary at the time of Ritchie's design being chosen. In 2003, endless international photographers snapped the Spire of Light as a symbol of Ireland's economic ascent. In recent years, foreign media outlets have instead been capturing demonstrations passing by Jim Larkin, his outstretched arms urging the Irish public into action.

There is certainly a nostalgic attitude towards the Nelson Pillar in Dublin today. We are still living in an age when many Dubliners can recall trips to its summit, and recount the views from the top and the experience of climbing its seemingly endless stairs. When Pete St. John penned 'The Rare Ould Times' in the 1970s, he wrote that:

> *The Pillar and the Met have gone,*
> *The Royal long since pulled down,*

As the grey unyielding concrete,
Makes a city of my town.[209]

To many Dubliners, the pillar and Nelson were very separate things. Many knew little, or cared little, of navy battles in the late eighteenth and early nineteenth centuries. To them, the pillar was a valued view over their own ever-changing city.

Yet, others did welcome his downfall, or at least didn't shed any tears. Reports of crowds cheering as the army carried out their controlled demolition in the aftermath of the republican bomb indicate that the attitude at the time, for many, was a light-hearted one.

The bombing of monuments in Ireland was not restricted to republican groups. In December 1969, a bomb on O'Connell Street did minor damage to the Daniel O'Connell monument. The action was later claimed by the Ulster Volunteer Force. In 1971, loyalists planted a bomb at St Stephen's Green, shattering Edward Delaney's monument to the Protestant republican figure Theobald Wolfe Tone. These blasts were every bit as capable of injuring innocent bystanders, and demonstrated that both militarist traditions could engage in a war over iconography. Republicans and loyalists in Northern Ireland attacked memorials and monuments on many occasions, for example the 1973 bombing of the pillar dedicated to the memory of the Reverend George Walker in Derry by Irish republicans. Walker, an Orange hero, had gazed over the nationalist Bogside. Like Nelson, he looked down over an environment that in time was largely alien to him.

Born in the 1980s, I never climbed the steps of the Nelson Pillar. Indeed, my parents were children at the time it was shattered by the bomb Liam Sutcliffe has told us he planted. Yet it is something with which I have always felt a great familiarity, and something I often envision as I stroll past Ritchie's contemporary work. During the course of writing this work, I wondered if the removal of Nelson himself from his vantage poin would have been the ideal compromise, removing from the pillar the imperialistic symbolism that irritated Irish nationalists, while retaining the view over the city for natives and visitors alike.

It is my hope that this book has demonstrated to Dubliners the important role the Nelson Pillar played in Irish life through the generations, as an adored and detested (depending on the Dubliner) monument at the heart of our city.

Robert. Stephen ~ Russell on Top
of Nelsons column." June. 1959.

During the course of writing this work, I bought an old second-hand copy of *And Nelson on his Pillar*, a retrospective history of the Nelson Pillar that was published a decade after the explosion. Out of it fell this striking photograph of three children on top of the monument, and on the first page of the book were the words 'Robert, Stephen and Russell on top of Nelson's Column, June 1959'. To date, I have been unable to locate any of this trio, but the image captures a great shared moment of youth on top of the pillar.

Bibliography

Select Bibliography

Works consulted for this book are referenced within the footnotes, however this select bibliography will assist those who wish to carry out further research on the Pillar and the Dublin of its times.

Archival material of relevance contained within:

Dublin City Library and Archive
Irish Architectural Archive
Military Archives, Cathal Brugha Barracks
National Archives of Ireland (NAI)
National Library of Ireland (NLI)

Online resources consulted:

Come Here To Me- www.comeheretome.com
Dictionary of Irish Biography - www.dib.cambridge.org
History Ireland - www.historyireland.com
Oireachtas Archive - www.oireachtas.ie
Library Ireland - www.libraryireland.com
RTE Archives - www.rte.ie/archives

Newspapers:

An Phoblacht
Boston Evening Transcript
Evening Herald
Freeman's Journal
Galway Observer
Irish Independent
New York Tribune
New York Times
Sunday Independent
The Blue Shirt
The Irish Times
The Nation
The Times (London)
Weekly Irish Times

Magazines, journals and periodicals:

Dublin Historical Review
Dublin Opinion
History Ireland
Irish Arts Review
Irish Historical Studies
The Irish Builder
The Irish Monthly

Publications:

Existing works on the Nelson Pillar consulted:

Book Chapters:
Myles, F. 'Admiral Nelson: my part in his downfall' in J.
    Fenwick (ed.) *Lost and Found II: Rediscovering Ireland's
    Past* (Dublin, 2009)

Sullivan, M. G. 'Making and Breaking Public Sculpture, 1688–1929 ' in *Art Under Attack: Histories of British Iconoclasm* (London, 2013)

Talks and articles:

Henchy, P., 'Nelson's Pillar' in *Dublin Historical Record* (Vol. 10, No. 2)

Ó Riain, M., 'Nelson's Pillar' in *History Ireland* (Vol 6, No.4)

Killian, T., 'Exploding the Myth: The Truth About the Demolition of Nelson's Pillar' in *Newsletter of the International Militaria Collectors Club* (2009)

Books:

O'Regan, J. (ed.), *A Monument in the City* (Dublin, 1998)

Bolger, W. and Share, B., *And Nelson on his Pillar* (Dublin, 1976)

Kennedy, D., *Dublin's Fallen Hero* (Belfast, 2013)

Selected other published works consulted:

Bennett, G., *Nelson the Commander* (South Yorkshire, 2002)

Coogan, T. P., *The IRA* (New York 2002)

Clark, P. and Gillespie, R. (eds.), *Two Capitals: London and Dublin, 1500–1840* (Oxford, 2001)

Doyle, R., *A Star Called Henry* (London, 2008)

Gilbert, J.T., *A History of the City of Dublin* (Dublin, 1854)

Gillis, L., *The Fall of Dublin* (Cork, 2011)

Hanley, B. and Millar, S., *The Lost Revolution: The Story of the Official IRA and the Workers' Party* (Dublin, 2009)

Higgins, R., *Transforming 1916: Meaning, Memory and the Fiftieth Anniversary of the Easter Rising* (Cork, 2001)

Hopkins, F., *Rare Old Dublin: Heroes, Hawkers & Hoors* (Dublin, 2002)

Kilfeather, S. M., *Dublin: A Cultural History* (Oxford, 2005)

Kincaid, A., *Postcolonial Dublin: Imperial Legacies* (Minnesota, 2006)

Konstam, A., *Horatio Nelson* (Oxford, 2011),

Lee, C., *The Silent Traveller in Dublin* (London, 1953

McBride, I. (ed.), *History and Memory in Modern Ireland* (Cambridge, 2001)

McDowell, R. B., *Historical Essays 1938–2001* (Dublin, 2004)

Morris, G. I., *In Dublin's Fair City* (London, 1947)

O'Casey, S., *Three Dublin Plays: The Shadow of a Gunman, Juno and the Paycock, The Plough and the Stars* (Dublin, 1998)

Ryan, D., *Blasphemers & Blackguards: The Irish Hellfire Clubs* (Dublin, 2012)

Whelan, Y., *Reinventing Modern Dublin: Streetscape, Iconography and the Politics of Identity* (Dublin, 2003)

Wright, G. N., *An Historical Guide to Ancient and Modern Dublin* (London, 1821)

Endnotes

1   H. Andrews, J. Coleman, 'Luke Gardiner' in *Dictionary of Irish Biography* (Online edition at dib.cambridge.org).

2   E. Sheridan-Quartz, 'Dublin: Multi-Centred Metropolis', in. P. Clark and R. Gillespie (eds.), *Two Capitals: London and Dublin, 1500–1840* (Oxford, 2001), p. 270.

3   F. Hopkins, *Rare Old Dublin: Heroes, Hawkers & Hoors* (Dublin, 2002), p. 114.

4   S. M. Kilfeather, *Dublin: A Cultural History* (Oxford, 2005), p. 54.

5   S. J. Connolly, *Divided Kingdom: Ireland 1630–1800* (Oxford, 2008), p. cx.

6   W. Issacson, *Benjamin Franklin: An American Life* (New York, 2003), p. 259.

7   Whitelaw's survey was tragically lost for the most part in 1922, as it was held in the Public Records Office of the Four Courts. What he published in 1805 as *An essay on the population of Dublin being the result of an actual survey taken in 1798, with great care and precision, and arranged in a manner entirely new*, is now digitised. See http://comeheretome.com/2013/11/18/a-forgotten-dublin-census/

8   E. Sheridan-Quartz 'Dublin: Multi-Centred Metropolis', in. P. Clark and R. Gillespie (eds.), *Two Capitals: London and Dublin, 1500–1840* (Oxford, 2001), p. 268.

9   A. Kincaid, *Postcolonial Dublin: Imperial Legacies* (Minnesota, 2006), p.xxv.

10   M. Shaffrey, 'Sackville Street/O'Connell Street' in *Irish Arts Review 1988–1989/1990*, p. 145.

11   R. Usher, *Protestant Dublin, 1660–1760: Architecture and Iconography* (Hampshire, 2012), p. 118.

12   J. T. Gilbert, *A History of the City of Dublin, Vol. 1* (Dublin,1854), p. 19.

13   A. Jackson, *Buildings of Empire* (Oxford, 2013), p. 15.

14   Quoted in the John Van Nost entry in the *Dictionary of Irish Artists* (Dublin, 1913).

15   Quoted in J. T. Gilbert, *A History of the City of Dublin, Vol. 1* (Dublin, 1854), p. 20.

16   *Irish Independent*, 7 January 1926.

17   Y. Whelan, *Reinventing Modern Dublin: Streetscape, Iconography and the Politics of Identity* (Dublin, 2003), p. 18.

18   M. G. Sullivan, 'Making and Breaking Public Sculpture, 1688–1929' in *Art Under Attack: Histories of British Iconoclasm* (London, 2013), pp. 92–113, p. 102.

19   *Ibid.*

20   J. Hill, 'National Festivals, the State and "Protestant Ascendancy" in Ireland 1790–1829' in *Irish Historical Studies* (Vol.29, No.93), pp. 30–51, p. 33.

21   Image of King William III statue taken from *Ireland in Pictures* (Chicago, 1898).

22   Gilbert, *A History of the City of Dublin, Vol. 1,* p. 294.

23   G. N. Wright, *An Historical Guide to Ancient and Modern Dublin* (London, 1821), p. 260.

24   Lines taken from the Shan Van Vocht, a traditional song dating back to the period of the United Irish rebellion hopeful of French assistance in Ireland.

25   *The Times,* 2 October 1798.

26   T. Pakenham, *The Year of Liberty: The History of the Great Irish Rebellion of 1798* (London, 1992), p. 337.

27   G. Bennett, *Nelson the Commander* (South Yorkshire, 2002), p. 9.

28   A. Konstam, *Horatio Nelson* (Oxford, 2011), p. 55.

29   D. Ryan, *Blasphemers & Blackguards: The Irish Hellfire Clubs* (Dublin, 2012), p. 10.

30   M. Kenny, *The 1798 Rebellion: Photographs and Memorabilia from the National Museum of Ireland* (Dublin, 1996), p. 5.

31   Original Declaration of the United Irishmen, 1798.

32   R. B. McDowell, 'The Dublin Society of United Irishmen, 1791–4' in *Historical Essays 1938–2001* (Dublin, 2004), p. 109.

33   T. W. Moody, R. B. McDowell and C. J. Woods (eds.), *The Writings of Theobald Wolfe Tone, 1763–98, Vol. III* (Oxford, 2007), p. 463.

34   R. O'Donnell, *Robert Emmet and the 1798 Rebellion* (Dublin, 2003), p. 119.

35   J. Quinn, 'Edward Marcus Despard' in *Dictionary of Irish Biography* (online version: http://dib.cambridge.org/)

36   *Ibid.*

37   E. Bairnes, *History of the wars of the French revolution, from the breaking out of the war, in 1792, to the restoration of a general peace, in 1815 : comprehending the civil history of Great Britain and France, during that period* (London, 1817), p. 385.

38   *The Trial of Edward Marcus Despard, Esquire. for High Treason.* (London, 1803), p. 260.

39   N. H. Nicolas (ed.), *The Dispatches and Letters of Admiral Lord Viscount Nelson* (London, 1844), p. 128.

40   R. B. McDowell, 'Ireland and England' in *Historical Essays 1938–2001* (Dublin, 2004), pp. 126–127.

41   J. Ehrman, *The Younger Pitt, The Consuming Struggle* (California, 1996), p. 187.

42   J. Barrington, *Rise and Fall of the Irish Nation* (New York, 1896), p. 7. This influential work was first published in 1833. It, along with several of Barrington's other works, have thankfully been digitised and are available freely at www.archive.org.

43   J. O'Connell (ed.), T*he Select Speeches of Daniel O'Connell M.P.* (Dublin, 1867), p. 179.

44   Taken from the autobiography of Hope, digitised and available at http:// thejimmyhopestory.rushlightmagazine.com/. For information on James Hope, see S.Cronin's *A Man of the People: James Hope* (Dublin, 1964).

45   D. Kennedy, *Dublin's Fallen Hero* (Belfast, 2013), p. 25.

46   T. W. Moody, R. B. McDowell and C. J. Woods (eds.), *The Writings of Theobald Wolfe Tone, 1763–98, Vol. II* (Oxford, 1998), p. 394.

47   *Freeman's Journal*, 2 November 1805.

48   *The Times,* 7 November 1805.

49   G. Bennett, *Nelson the Commander* (New York, 2005), p. 285.

50   P. Dixon Hardy (ed.), *Dublin Penny Journal 1834–5 (Dublin, 1835),* p. 405.

51   The *Freeman's Journal*, 24 March 1808.

52   P. Henchy, 'Nelson's Pillar' in *Dublin Historical Record* (Vol. 10, No. 2), pp. 53–63, p. 53.

53   *Freeman's Journal*, 26 November 1805.

54   J. Joyce, *The Guinnesses: The Untold Story of Ireland's Most Successful Family* (Dublin, 2009), p. 40.

55   *The Times*, 21 April 1806.

56   Report on an 1807 meeting of the Committee held in Commercial Buildings, reprinted in W. Bolger, B. Share, *And Nelson on his Pillar*, (Dublin, 1976), p. 16.

57   *Ibid.* p. 24.

58   *Nelson's Pillar; A Description of the Pillar with a list of subscribers, etc. to which is Added, the Amount of the Funds, and the Account of the Expenditure Thereof* (Dublin, 1846).

59   G. N. Wright, *An Historical Guide to Ancient and Modern Dublin*, p. 266.

60   F. O'Dwyer, 'Francis Johnston' in *Dictionary of Irish Biography* (online version: http://dib.cambridge.org/)

61   Thomas Kirk entry in W. G. Strickland's *Dictionary of Irish Artists* (Dublin, 1913).

62   *Nelson's Pillar; A Description of the Pillar with a list of subscribers, etc. to which is Added, the Amount of the Funds, and the Account of the Expenditure Thereof* (Dublin, 1846).

63   *Freeman's Journal,* 28 August 1809.

64   *Freeman's Journal,* 12 August 1809.

65   *Irish Monthly Magazine,* 1809.

66   R. Walsh, J. Warburton and J. Whitelaw, *History of the City of Dublin: From the Earliest Accounts to the Present Time… Vol. II* (London, 1818), pp. 1101–1102.

67   M. G. Sullivan, 'Making and Breaking Public Sculpture, 1688–1929' in *Art Under Attack: Histories of British Iconoclasm* (London, 2013), pp. 92–113, p. 110.

68   This *Irish Monthly Magazine* attack on the pillar is quoted in A. Tucker's *Moving Through Modernity: Space and Geography in Modernism* (Manchester, 2003), p. 122.

69   Entry on Walter Cox in A. Webb, *A Compendium of Irish Biography* (Dublin, 1878), digitised at www.libraryireland.com.

70   This description is taken from an anonymous work entitled *Account of the Celebration of the Jubilee* (Birmingham, 1809), p. 200.

71   D. Dickson, 'Death of a capital? Dublin and the consequences of Union' in P. Clarke, R. Gillespie (eds.) *Two Capitals: London and Dublin, 1500–1840* (Oxford, 2001), pp. 111–132, p. 131.

72   L. Colantonio, 'Democracy and the Irish People, 1830–48' in J. Innes, M. Philip (eds.), *Re-imagining Democracy in the Age of Revolutions: America, France, Britain, Ireland 1750–1850* (Oxford, 2013), pp. 162–173, p. 163.

73   Frederick Douglass, *The Life and Times of Frederick Douglass* (New York, 2003), p. 168.

74   *The Irish Times,* 7 October 1862.

75   *The Irish Times,* 13 May 1876.

76   'Nelson's Pillar (Dublin) Bill', Private Business in House of Commons, 13 February 1891.

77   *Irish Builder,* 15 April 1894.

78   *Freeman's Journal,* 4 June 1881.

79   *The Irish Times,* 28 July 1917.

80   *Irish Independent,* 21 October 1905.

81   *The Irish Times,* 28 Oct October 1805.

82   *Ibid.*

83   'Political affiliation of council members' chart in J. V. O'Brien, *Dear, Dirty Dublin: A City In Distress* (California, 1982), p. 93.

84   *Report of the Dublin Disturbances Commission* (London, 1914). Available online at http://multitext.ucc.ie/d/Report_of_the_Dublin_Disturbances_Commission_1914.

85   I. McBride, 'Memory and National Identity in Modern Ireland', I. McBride (ed.) *History and Memory in Modern Ireland* (Cambridge, 2001), pp. 1–42, p. 30.

86   *Freeman's Journal,* 9 August 1864.

87   *The Nation* newspaper spearheaded a campaign against the Prince Albert monument when College Green was suggested as a location for it. This

campaign ran in April and May of 1864. There were protests at meetings of the Corporation and in the Rotunda, some involving Fenians.

88   *Freeman's Journal,* 9 August 1898.

89   Dublin Corporation Minutes 1898, No. 287 (Dublin City Library and Archives, Pearse Street).

90   *The Irish Times,* 17 February 1908.

91   Letter from John Wilson Croker to the Secretary of the Wellington Fund, 7 October 1814. Contained within L. J. Jennings (ed.), *The Croker Papers: The correspondence and diaries of the late Right Honourable John Wilson Croker, secretary to the admiralty from 1809 to 1830* (London, 1885), p. 58.

92   *Boston Evening Transcript,* 2 October 1911.

93   *Derry People,* 7 October 1911.

94   These words are attributed to Patrick Pearse in the General Post Office. They are quoted in Desmond Ryan's memoirs of being inside the GPO, and in other contemporary sources.

95   T. Coffey, *Agony at Easter: The 1916 Irish Uprising* (Baltimore, 1971), p. 21.

96   A letter written by Michael Collins from Frongoch internment camp, quoted in T. P. Coogan's *Michael Collins: The Man Who Made Ireland* (New York, 1990), p. 54.

97   Sean T. O'Kelly, Bureau of Military History Witness Statement W.S 1765.

98   E. O'Malley, *On Another Man's Wound* (Colorado, 2001), p.31.

99   *Sinn Féin Rebellion Handbook* (Dublin, 1917). This rather sensationalist account of the uprising was published in 1917 by *The Irish Times.* It has been digitised in full at: https://archive.org/details/sinnfeinrebellio00dubl.

100   T. Coffey, *Agony at Easter* (New York, 1971), p. 41.

101   *The Irish Times,* 13 May 1916.

102   Sean MacEntee, Bureau of Military History Witness Statement W.S 1052.

103   Liam Tannam, Bureau of Military History Witness Statement W.S 242.

104   Joseph McDonagh, Bureau of Military History Witness Statement W.S 1082.

105   Ina Heron, Bureau of Military History Witness Statement W.S 919.

106   *New York Tribune,* 1 May 1916.

107   S. O'Casey, *Three Dublin Plays: The Shadow of a Gunman, Juno and the Paycock, The Plough and the Stars* (Dublin, 1998), p. 205.

108   R. Doyle, *A Star Called Henry* (London, 2008), p. 128.

109   R. Jeffs, *Brendan Behan: Man and Showman* (London, 1968), p. 117.

110   Newspaper reported quoted in L. Gillis, *The Fall of Dublin* (Cork, 2011), p. 100.

111   *Ibid.,* p. 108.

112   *The Irish Times,* 12 November 1926.

113   J. Joyce, *Ulysses* (First published in 1922. Oxford, 1993), p. 142.

114 *Ibid.*, p.15.
115 *The Irish Times*, 18 July 1925.
116 Correspondence held within Department of An Taoiseach, files at National Archives of Ireland, NAI S/4523.
117 Newspaper clipping in same archival source, NAI S/4523.
118 *The Irish Times*, 12 December 1931.
119 Dáil Éireann Debate, Vol.117 No.2, 6 July 1949.
120 The remarks of W. B. Yeats were quoted in M. Ó Riain, 'Nelson's Pillar' in *History Ireland*, Vol 6, No.4 (Winter, 1996).
121 *The Blueshirt*, 1 March 1935.
122 *Evening Herald*, 12 December 1931.
123 *The Irish Times*, 28 December 1931.
124 *The Irish Times*, 6 October 1937.
125 *The Irish Times*, 28 January 1961.
126 Correspondence held within Department of An Taoiseach files at National Archives of Ireland, NAI S/4523.
127 *Ibid.*
128 M. O'Riordan remarks at SIPTU conference, 11 October 2002.
129 B. Hanley, '"A man the ages will remember." Mike Quill, the TWU and Civil Rights' in *History Ireland*, (Vol.12, No.4).
130 *The Irish Times*, 22 January 1964.
131 *Irish Independent*, 30 October 1955.
132 G. I. Morris, *In Dublin's Fair City* (London, 1947), p. 38.
133 J. Harvey, *Dublin* (London, 1949), p. 31.
134 C. Lee, *The Silent Traveller in Dublin* (London, 1953), p. 23.
135 Transcript held within Department of An Taoiseach files at National Archives of Ireland, NAI S/4523.
136 Behan's remarks about the pillar here were first published after his death, in *Confessions of an Irish Rebel*, released in 1965.
137 M. O'Sullivan, *Brendan Behan: A Life* (Colorado, 1999), p. 70.
138 A. Clarke, 'Nelson's Pillar, Dublin' in *Too Great a Vine* (Dublin, 1957).
139 *The Irish Times*, 19 November 1955.
140 *Galway Observer*, 27 May 1922.
141 *The Irish Times*, 12 November 1928.
142 *The Irish Times*, 11 December 1928.
143 *The Irish Times*, 22 May 1937.
144 *The Irish Times*, 12 November 1937.
145 *The Irish Times*, 20 February 1933.
146 *The Irish Times*, 10 May 1951.
147 Tim Pat Coogan, *The IRA* (New York, 2002), p.120.
148 *Ibid.*
149 V. Caprani, 'The Ballad of Gough' in *Rowdy Rhymes and reci-im-itations* (Dublin, 2007).

150 This song was sung in RTÉs *Scannal* Documentary on the Nelson Pillar. See www.rte.ie/tv/scannal/nelsonspillar.html.

151 *The Irish Times,* 27 August 1958.

152 *The Irish Times,* 31 October 1955.

153 *The Irish Times,* 5 November 1955.

154 'Nelson's Pillar (Dublin): damage caused by University College Dublin students' in National Archives of Ireland, JUS/8/1030.

155 'Nelson's Pillar (Dublin): damage caused by University College Dublin students', National Archives of Ireland, JUS/8/1030.

156 *Ibid.*

157 *The Irish Times,* 19 November 1955.

158 *Irish Independent,* 28 November 1955.

159 *The Irish Times,* 9 March 1966.

160 While RTÉ is unable to provide an original date of airing for the Nelson Pillar feature, it has been digitised at: www.rte.ie/archives/.

161 R. Higgins, *Transforming 1916: Meaning, Memory and the Fiftieth Anniversary of the Easter Rising* (Cork, 2001), p. 76.

162 *The Irish Times,* 9 March 1966.

163 *The Irish Times,* 10 March 1966.

164 *The Irish Times,* 9 March 1966.

165 *Irish Independent,* 9 March 1966.

166 *The Economist* was quoted in *The Irish Times,* 17 March 1966.

167 *Irish Press,* 9 March 1966.

168 *Morning Record,* 9 March 1966.

169 Nelson Pillar Bill debate in Seanad Éireann, 23 April 1969.

170 T. Killian, 'Exploding the Myth: The Truth About the Demolition of Nelson's Pillar' in *Newsletter of the International Militaria Collectors Club,* 2009 edition.

171 *Irish Independent,* 9 March 1966.

172 F. Myles, 'Admiral Nelson: my part in his downfall' in J. Fenwick (ed.) *Lost and Found II. Rediscovering Ireland's Past* (Dublin, 2009) pp. 303–313, p. 312.

173 R. White, 'Ruairí Ó Brádaigh: The Life and Politics of an Irish Revolutionary (Indiana, 2006), p. 58.

174 L. W. W. White, 'Joseph Christle' in *Dictionary of Irish Biography* (online version: http://dib.cambridge.org/).

175 B. Hanley, S. Millar, *The Lost Revolution: The Story of the Official IRA and the Workers' Party* (Dublin, 2009).

176 *The Irish Times,* 22 January 2003.

177 A video interview with Liam, entitled 'Liam Sutcliffe: Irish Republican, Solider and Revolutionary', is available to view at http://www.youtube.com/watch?v=XqqRgIdBDAM.

178 *The Irish Times,* 21 September 2000.

179 Emmet Grogan's book is considered a classic account of the American hippy movement of the 1960s, but it also contains great insight into Dublin. Fact and fiction are often blurred, and in the words of *The New Yorker*, 'Mr. Grogan writes so clearly that he almost convinces us that the whole story could be true.'

180 *The Times*, 21 April 1966.

181 *Sunday Independent*, 13 March 1966.

182 *Irish Press*, 19 March 1966.

183 Ó Duibhir has documented this bizarre incident on his personal historical site: http://photopol.com/nelson_show/head.html.

184 *Irish Press*, 18 April 1966.

185 *The Times*, 18 April 1966.

186 *Irish Press*, 2 May 1966.

187 *Sing*, Vol.9 No.2, June 1966.

188 R. Higgins, *Transforming 1916* (Cork, 2013), p. 76.

189 Nelson Pillar Bill debate in Seanad Éireann, 23 April 1969.

190 Y. Whelan, *Reinventing Modern Dublin* (Dublin, 2003), p. 162.

191 *Guardian*, 6 September 1999.

192 *The Irish Times*, 25 March 1987.

193 *The Irish Times*, 5 March 1988.

194 Y. Whelan, *Reinventing Modern Dublin*, p. 238.

195 *A Monument in the City*, p. 33.

196 *Ibid.*, p. 42.

197 *Ibid.*, p. 52.

198 *Ibid.*, p. 50.

199 *The Irish Times*, 25 March 1993.

200 *The Irish Times*, 29 March 1996.

201 *The Irish Times*, 18 March 1996.

202 *The Irish Times*, 26 November 1998.

203 M. P. Corcoran, 'Place Remaking in Dublin' in M. P. Corcoran, M. Peillon (eds.) *Place and Non-Place: The Reconfiguration of Ireland (Dublin, 2004)*, pp. 142–156.

204 A. Garvey, 'Competition row brews over Ritchie's Dublin steel spire' on www.ArchitectsJournal.co.uk, 27 May 1999.

205 *Irish Independent*, 24 July 1999.

206 *The Irish Times*, 24 June 2000.

207 F. Myles, 'Admiral Nelson: my part in his downfall' in J. Fenwick (ed.) *Lost and Found II. Rediscovering Ireland's Past* (Dublin, 2009), pp. 303–313, p. 311.

208 *The Irish Times*, 23 January 2003.

209 Lyrics by Pete St. John. See www.petestjohn.com.